Robert Thornton was born in Dublin in 1944 and grew up and went to school there until the age of 15. He moved to Kent, England, in 1959, where he continued his education part-time between different career choices, including engineering apprenticeship, washing machine salesman, debt collector, military (three years) and eventually, schoolteacher and headmaster. He lives in Somerset with his wife, Veronica.

To my 11 brothers and sisters, and to the memory of my sister,
Peggy (1954–1958).

Robert Thornton

SLEEP WITH THE HOLY GHOST

AUSTIN MACAULEY PUBLISHERS™

LONDON * CAMBRIDGE * NEW YORK * SHARJAH

A CIP catalogue record for this title is available from the British Library.

ISBN 9781035835478 (Paperback)
ISBN 9781035835485 (ePub e-book)

www.austinmacauley.com

First Published 2024
Austin Macauley Publishers Ltd®
1 Canada Square
Canary Wharf
London
E14 5AA

Terry and Marie Osborne for their encouragement to publish.

I would also like to express my gratitude to the following sources for providing me with the images for my book cover.

Front cover photographs clockwise from top:

- Fagan children with their father.
- Anne Frank—photo courtesy of Anne Frank House, Amsterdam.
- The Evacuation of Jews—photo courtesy of Truman Library, Independence, Missouri, USA.
- The Old Coombe Hospital, Dublin. Drawing by Michael O'Brien from Me Jewel and Darlin' Dublin by Éamonn MacThomáis, published by The O'Brien Press Ltd. Copyright © the estate of Michael O'Brien.

Chapter 1

His brother, Denis, had soiled himself again. His short brown corduroy trousers were weeping the awful evidence; his shape in walking was bandy cowboy. He was offended by the smell of him as they walked along the bank of the Dodder, keeping an eye on the trout pools on the far side under the over-hanging branches. He felt sorry for him.

Trouts can pee or poo anywhere just like birds and chickens and all, and nobody cares. Da'll hose him down again in the yard. He hates that. The water'll be frozen, and the others will be laughing their arses off. And he won't just hose the shite off him; he'll go for him everywhere, in his mouth and in his mickey and Da doesn't realise that when he gets a good aim in the mickey, it hurts like shaggin hell. It's funny the way animals don't wear clothes.

They've got more sense. They can do a shite anywhere and they don't dirty their trousers. I suppose if you had those underpants on it'd be better. But you have to be posh to have underpants. Like those Protestants who live at the bottom of our street. They're English as well. They're from a town called Newcastle in the north of England and they speak in posh voices.

They don't say you have to wash up the plates and saucers and cups and all, like we do; they just say you have to mend the pots and pans. There are more posh Protestant people in England than in Ireland. "The greatest country in the world, England," that's what my Da says. I said to Da that I'd heard somebody say that England was Ireland's enemy.

"Don't you listen to those shaggin eegits! They're like little poodles barking at a big Alsatian—all mouth and swagger. Ireland's enemy my arse."

They had reached the waterfall and he stopped and looked at Denis who was trying hard to put his disgrace out of his mind and what his mother would do to him, let alone his father. He knew his father would give him a good lick of the hose as well, as if being older made him responsible for his brother's bowels.

The water in the river was peaty brown and foaming at the base of the weir and the boy could feel the spume on his face. He turned and looked up into the sun, still high in the late afternoon, and then over the roofs of houses to the Dublin Mountains only five or six miles away. His gaze stayed on the Hell Fire Club on the top of the central ridge.

I'll go and live in the mountains; that's what I'll do. And Da won't be able to get me. And I'll be able to wash in the bog pools when I like, and with all them sheep up there, you'd never go hungry, though I don't like washing that much. And I don't know if I'd be able to kill a sheep. "Slaughter" is the word they use—the butchers and all.

"Have a good wash behind your ears for your birthday," that's what Ma said. Only two weeks ago, and I was ten, it was my birthday and Ma and Da thought I was great.

We went to the pictures and saw Goodbye Mr Chips. *I thought that was great especially when the kid was walking along the corridor throwing his apple in the air and catching it coming down, and another kid, bigger than him, comes along and he catches the apple and slams it into his gob and takes a huge chunk out of it and then gives it back. Jesus, I nearly fell off the seat laughing and Ma telling me to stop laughing as I was disturbing other people.*

We've got funny names for our picture houses, awful shaggin names really. "The Landscape", "The Kenilworth", "The Stella", "The Princess", "The De Luxe". When Tony went to England last year to stay with Aunt Margie, he told us they call them "cinemas" and they had names like "The Ritz" and "The Regent", "The Odeon" and "The Gaumont", and what's more, he said they used the same names for the cinemas no matter what town you were in.

Now, that makes a lot of sense because then you don't have to think up loads of new names every time you want to call a cinema something and anyway who ever thought to call a picture house "The Landscape", it just doesn't sound right. They're definitely posher in England.

He turned again to gaze at the water exploding into the bottom of the weir. His friend, Reddy, had told him that the water in the weir was foamy and brown because of all the Guinness porter that was drunk in Dublin and all the men having a pee on the way home from the pubs; but he did not believe him for he knew that the river came from a spring in the mountains and flowed down through the peat bogs taking on its lovely brownish colour before finding the city and the sea. He went with his father often when not in school to the turf cuttings in the Dublin hills where his father had some holdings.

He loved to be with him, especially going through the pine forests before they reached the tree line and the bare wilderness of the bogs. He felt a slight shiver whenever they passed the dull grey, unfriendly building known as the Hell Fire Club.

'Where did it get that name, Da?'

'Well, the story has it that a crowd of young bucks from Dublin—aristocrats they were—used to come up from the city in their carriages and do all sorts of wild things. This was a long time ago, in the middle of the 18th century or so.'

'What sort of wild things, Da?'

'Oh, they gambled and got drunk and had wild parties, and all that class of thing with debaucheries and everything.'

'What does debaucheries mean?'

'Well, it means messing about with women and things like that. Anyway, will you let me explain as you asked the question. One night, a particularly bad night, the story goes as far as the debauching and swilling the porter and knocking back the short ones was concerned…didn't the auld devil himself come and visit their nibs while they were up to no particular good.'

'There was panic at the sight of him as he had his goat's horns and head on as well as his pig's feet; people were running everywhere and knocking things over and getting in each other's way. Pandemonium broke out.'

'What's panemonia, Da?'

'Never mind. The point is that a fire started and people were mad to escape, not just the fire but the devil himself, who by this time had installed himself high up in the roof timbers and who was killing himself laughing at the poor unfortunate eegits below. The laugh was horrible itself and people who looked up into his eyes—direct mind you—died on the spot.'

A loud, mocking and harsh voice clattered into the boy's daydreaming.

'Well, will you look at yourself, Dinny Fagan; your auld fella will beat the living shite out of you when you get home.'

'There's no living shite left in me, Mr Brophy,' answered Denis.

'God help your mammy having to wash them trousers that's all I can say, you little pantaloon, can you not control yourself for Christ's sake? Get him home, Patsy, before the smell kills us.'

Patsy Fagan, for that was his name, looked at Mr Brophy's black Ford Prefect pulling away and he knew of the very strong probability that they would all know of his brother's mishap before they ever reached home. Mrs Brophy had asked him and Denis in the school holidays if they would like to come and clear the rubbish out of the garden. Patsy was waiting to hear what the wages might be and Mrs Brophy seemed to read his mind.

'We'll have tea and cake and all,' she reassured him.

On their way home, Denis asked his brother what Mrs Brophy meant by "and all".

'She can stick her tea and cake "and all" up her arse as well as her garden.'

Patsy had two brothers and two sisters. He was the second born; Tony, the eldest, was fourteen months his senior; his sister, Eileen, was a year younger than himself, and Denis, known as Dinny, three years younger. Finally, but not for long, as their mother was pregnant again, came the youngest, Alana, aged 4. She was Patsy's favourite and his special care. His parents and the other children knew this preference, and if asked to explain, they would probably have said it was to be expected as Alana was the youngest, the baby, and it was natural to spoil her.

Patsy would not have agreed but would have found it difficult to give a better answer. A neighbour or a relation would, no doubt, have said that it was because Alana had been born a cripple. She was entirely paralysed from the waist down, had a turnip-size hump on her back and an overly large head. She had no control over her bladder or bowel functions at all and she was fully dependent on others to manage all her bodily needs.

It was Patsy who mainly looked after her and who loved her fiercely. It was not that her parents or her other brothers and sister loved her less or were reluctant to care for her; it was a simple recognition that fate somehow or other had marked Patsy out to be her special friend.

She was exceptionally bright and always cheerful, and ever keen to play and sing. Patsy helped her learn to read, and by the age of 4, she could manage more than simple sentences.

'How are you me auld Alana?' he'd shout when he got in from school.

'Come and sit here, Patsy,' she'd beam back.

'Wait till I get a piece of bread and I'll come and talk to you.'

'Patsy, bring me a bit of bread with sugar and butter on it.'

'You always say "with sugar and butter" but the butter comes first so you should say "with butter and sugar", now will you learn that.'

Patsy would bury his dark curly head gently into her belly and make her scream with delight by burrowing backwards and forwards with his head and by putting his lips to her bared chest and blowing big wet raspberries.

'Turn me over on to me other side, Patsy, please.'

'Aren't you an awful shaggin nuisance. There you are now…is that OK?'

'Patsy, sing Daisy and move me to the other side. Can we go to the park in the pram tomorrow?'

And so the boy and his sister carried on. She had her place on the couch in the living room and could go nowhere else without being carried; nor could she shift her position on the couch without help. When it wasn't cold outside, she would lie for hours in her pram in the backyard waiting for her mother or father to come and kiss her, pet her and make a fuss over her, which they did a great deal.

'We're going now, Ma. We're going. Do you hear, Ma, we're going. We'll be back early.'

'Don't be bold and look after Alana and keep her warm, and don't go running with the pram. Do yous hear me, Tony? Patsy, do yous hear me?'

'Yes, Ma.'

They could no more not run with the pram than not breathe. They flew yelping and shouting along the roads like Geronimo and Crazy Horse in the cowboy pictures, slapping their imaginary horses on the rump to get more speed. Often on these excursions with the cowboys in flight and the Indians in pursuit, the slopes and bends on the paths in the park proved too much for their stagecoach, and Alana's pram would go spinning out of control and topple over spilling everything within, including the unfortunate child, onto the gravel path.

Everybody listened for the silence to end and only came back to life when the crippled girl burst the air with her cries. Then the young Roy Rogers or

Hopalong Cassidy would run to her and scrabble her up in arms and look for signs of serious injury and kiss her, hold her, hug her and beg her not to say anything to Ma or Da who could not bear the thought of their tiny darling being hurt.

Although only 10, Patsy took the responsibility of bathing his sister. He would carry her to the sink or use a kitchen basin. He had to be careful when he flannelled the areas around her heels and knees for fear of removing flesh from the bone. More often than not, the skin and flesh in these areas were badly damaged and required constant attention. Patsy often helped his mother to dress these open, deep wounds with the sterilised gauze pads, which came in tins from the chemist's shop.

She died just before her sixth birthday. The doctor said her little heart could no longer support her large head.

'She was an angel lent to us by God,' her dad said.

'We're giving her back to the angels and we'll all see her again when we leave this world.' That's what the priest said at her funeral.

Patsy had walked in the rain-soaked funeral procession with his brothers and sister Eileen, trying not to show he was crying. His uncle Bill was beside him soothing; 'There now Patsy wipe your tears.'

And Patsy with brave face, tried a smile.

'I'm alright but I didn't have a black coat to wear, only this shaggin white mac.'

The pain and hurt of Alana's death seeped deeply into the hearts of her parents and brothers and sister. Their spirits were dulled and their senses deadened despite the efforts of neighbours and friends to distract and encourage them. It was Nuala Fagan's pregnancy and the anticipation of a new baby that gradually forced the children's father to try to bring normality back to the household.

'Rise and shine, gentlemen. Eileen! Are you awake?' her father called in a gleeful and triumphant voice.

He took great pride in being first up every morning and rejoiced in not needing an alarm clock.

'Those things are only for sissies or for people who are too lazy to wake up. Your Da has never needed one of those. Up, gentlemen, up! Eileen, are you up?'

The morning was cold but the house was warm from the big storage heater in the hall, which glowed frighteningly red at night but mercifully did not set fire to the house or cause serious burn to anyone. Each morning, their father prepared their breakfast, usually porridge and bread and butter. In the winter, he ministered to each a spoonful of cod liver oil from a large gallon-size jar that appeared each year from some source which remained a mystery to the children. Their mother received her cup of tea from her husband in bed every morning, where she was seldom without an infant to nurse.

'That's where I used to go to school, Dinny, when I was small.'

'You tell me that every time we pass by. It really gets on me nerves. I went there too but I don't say, that's where I used to go to school, Patsy, when I was small, like a bloody eegit.'

'That's because you're still small,' Patsy answered with good humour.

The two brothers were on their way to the Boys' National School in Milltown where they had been from the age of 7 and which they would leave at 13 or 14 to go to work unless a scholarship came along or their father could afford the fees in a private school. Patsy, as he always did, looked over the low wall and through the windows of his old infant school, hopeful of spotting Sister Carmel. He had started school in Marymount when he was 4.

Tony and he had started school on the same day but Tony had not been afraid, being older than Patsy, who was crying in the schoolyard wanting only to go home to his mother, when the nun came out and rang a bell for everybody to come into class. His mother had told him to be brave and he would soon get used to it and wouldn't it be wonderful when he could read.

'My name is Sister Carmel and I want you all to learn a beautiful prayer called The Angelus. Now, after me, repeat the words:

The angel of the Lord declared unto Mary.
And she conceived by the Holy Ghost.'

Forty little children's voices murmured, or voiced confidently, the nun's words. Patsy was amongst the murmurers.

'Behold the handmaid of the Lord.
Be it done unto me according to thy word.
Hail Mary full of grace…'

At 12.00 noon every day, the ritual took place in the classroom and Sister Carmel put her ears close to her pupils' mouths to listen and to be sure they knew their prayers correctly.

'She always smiles at me when she listens to me saying The Angelus.'

'I wonder why that should be,' his mother answered.

'I can't help it, Mrs Fagan,' explained Sister Carmel after Mass one Sunday, 'but I wouldn't have him change it for all the tea in China.'

'What is it?' Patsy's mother asked.

'Well, your fella Patsy isn't satisfied with saying, "The angel of the Lord declared unto Mary and she conceived by the Holy Ghost". Oh no, the bold Patsy Fagan says, "The angel of the Lord declared unto Mary and she can sleep with the Holy Ghost"!'

There were few smiles when it came to Sister Agnes and learning to sing hymns.

'We're practising Soul of my Saviour today, children, and I will not accept any boy or girl praising Our Lord half-heartedly. I hope you all understand me…do you?'

'Yes, Sister Agnes.'

Patsy liked singing but not for Sister Agnes.

She's always looking to get you. She's got a big beaky nose that can just smell if there's anything wrong. It's like an arrow that's going to stick in you. I like Sister Carmel because she's got a lovely face, like a rosy apple with little cuts in it for the mouth and eyes and things.

He did not hear the swish of the bamboo cane before it lashed across the backs of his legs. The pain shot through his whole body and the tears welled up in his eyes but the crying choked in his mouth and he held himself and bit his lips to stop the sounds escaping.

'I'll give you tapping your foot when you're singing to Our Lord, you little blackguard. Keep your legs and feet still or I'll lash them off you.'

His friend, Gurky Ryan, said he should have told her he had a musical leg that moved on its own when the singing started. When Patsy's younger brother, Dinny, came home from Marymount with the red welt of a bamboo cane across the cheek of his face and blood oozing from the stroke received on his leg, their father lost his customary tolerance of the clergy, male and female.

'I'll wring her bloody fuckin neck, I will.'

'You ought to be ashamed of yourself, Tom Fagan, swearing like that in front of the children, and cursing and blinding a nun, a bride of Christ herself,' said his wife, Nuala.

'By Jesus Christ! By His blood on the Holy Cross! Will you look at Dinny, will you look at his face? What sort of evil bitch can she be to send the poor god-forsaken little fella home like that? And for what? Because he writes with his left hand! What sort of fuckin bride of Christ is she to do that? You'd know she's never suckled a baby if the evil rotten horse-faced pig can do such a thing.'

'Well, God forgive you for such blasphemy, Tom Fagan. Taking Our Lord's name in vain in such a disgraceful manner in front of young children. Patsy, Dinny, get off to bed and don't wake Eileen. Thank God, she's in bed and your brother Tony is staying with his aunt Peggy so they don't have to hear the terrible sins that are going on in this house tonight.'

Patsy listened to the row between his parents and prayed desperately to God to make them stop. His mother was crying, and his father's anger was becoming worse, and he hated Sister Agnes with all the futility that a 7 year old child can muster. He tried to drown the sounds his parents were making by pulling up the blankets over his head but in vain.

'You'll have to go to confession to Father McKenna on Friday night and ask forgiveness for your blasphemy.'

Tom Fagan was in no mood for asking priests for forgiveness.

'Well, by Jesus Christ this takes the biscuit; me little son is destroyed by a hard-faced, ignorant fucker of some farmer's daughter from the arsehole of the country no doubt, and me wife is begging me to go to confession to another fat-arsed gobshite who is nothing more than a rotten culchie ballocks himself.'

Nuala wilted under the onslaught of her husband.

'I'll pray for you, Tom Fagan, and ask God to forgive you for your bad work this night.'

'You can ask him, Nuala, to forgive all the vicious couldn't-give-a-fuck for the poor of this country priests and nuns who live off the fat of the land in their grand houses and convents. And you can include in that the Arch-stinking-bishop of Dublin and that long Spaniard-American culchie who lords it over the country, and who won't hear a word of criticism against the bastards. And I'll tell you something more; if one of them ever harms one of my children again, I'll wring their disgusting bloody necks.'

Chapter 2

There were no nuns or priests at Milltown but Patsy knew there were other forms of torture.

'Tell me, Fagan, how much is seven times thirty-nine?'

'I'll come up there and show you how to work it out for yourself, Mr Bambrick,' answered Patsy, looking for a laugh.

'Come up here alright, Fagan, and I'll show you how I work out my new cane. You're very lucky it's not the deluxe model, just the poor old standard three-footer; still, it's very good for teaching smart alecks to mind their manners on a Monday morning. Is that you sniggering, Gurky Ryan? It is; ah sure, you can come and join the party as well. Both hands now, lads, four on each. Aren't yous dead lucky that I'm feeling generous today and not going to give yous six on each hand? How much is four times six, Fagan?'

'Twenty-four, Sir.'

'Four times four, Ryan?'

'Sixteen, Sir.'

'That's much better now, isn't it?'

Patsy, sitting at his desk working out the twenty sums Mr Bambrick had put on the blackboard, was feeling a little sorry for himself, but unlike Sister Agnes, whom he still hated after all these years, he was fond of Mr Bambrick and his sarcastic ways.

'I just like the way he comes in the morning and he lights his cigarette and puts the sums on the board and just gets on with it.'

'But he doesn't do anything…just smokes,' added Reddy Costello.

'What's wrong with that?' Patsy argued. 'He comes in, puts the sums up, gets his pack of Gold Flake out, lights up, sits down at his table, puts up his feet, gets out his Irish Times and starts reading. He just leaves you alone.'

'Anyway,' Gurky Ryan said, 'he teaches yous good sums; they're not like the shaggin things that me sister, Brenda, gets up in the Loretta Convent that nobody can do. They must be awful feckin eegits giving you sums you can't do. I think auld Bambo's got his head screwed on right, giving you sums you can do and you can get them right. That makes much more sense, doesn't it?'

'I love the way Mr Welsh reads the Shakespeare stuff,' Patsy told his friend, Gurky, as they walked home through the Milltown golf course.

'I never understand it, Patsy; what do you love about it?'

'I love his voice and the words and the feelings that I get inside me and the things I hear in me head when he says his favourite bits and all.'

'I think I know what you mean.'

Patsy did not know what he meant himself, but he knew he could not stop listening when the teacher read his selected lines. He could not help the echo in his head and could see in his mind his own script.

Mr Welsh: **'*I come to bury Caesar, not to praise him.*'**

Patsy: '*I come to praise Alana, not to bury her.*'

Mr Welsh: '***Now is the winter of our discontent, made Glorious summer by this sudden sun of York.***'

Patsy: '*Now is the winter of my discontent made awful by my little sister's death.*'

Mr Welsh: '***Eyes, look your last.***'

Patsy: '*Eyes that shall never see again.*'

Mr Welsh: '***Arms, take your last embrace.***'

Patsy: '*Arms that will never go around my neck again.*'

Mr Welsh: '***And lips, oh thou the doors of breath.***'

Patsy: '*Lips that will never smile and sing again.*'

Mr Welsh: '***Seal with a righteous kiss a dateless bargain to engrossing death.***'

Patsy: '*Give us a kiss, Alana, and I'll get you a bit of bread and sugar and butter.*'

The class went to see a film version of *Romeo and Juliet* in the Carlton Cinema, organised by Mr Welsh, and Patsy's head was full of burning passion for all hard done by adolescent girls. He was Romeo, the lover, and at the same time, Robin Hood, stoutly defending the poor with his trusty bow and arrows. He was also Roy Rogers, King of the cowboys, with his white hat and fast draw.

The end of every adventure for him was to hold the virtuous maiden in his noble arms or to ride off into the sunset astride his faithful steed.

The deaths of Romeo and Juliet were for him a temporary hitch on their way to eternal bliss; it was a riding into the sunset, but as in the pictures, it was the beginning of everlasting, pure and lofty love, not simply the end of the story.

He was not altogether ready for the rather different impact the film had on his best friends.

'Jesus, did yous see the diddies bursting out of the top of her dress on that Juliet?' Gurky Ryan asked.

'You're right,' added Reddy Costello. 'I didn't understand a shaggin word, but she was gorgeous. Who was the quare fellow playing Romeo?'

'I don't know,' answered Gurky Ryan. 'I wasn't watching him; I was watching her and her diddies. It's an awful pity though you can't understand what they're saying. Why don't they speak in a proper language like us?'

Patsy could not remain silent. His young soul would not allow any vulgarity towards Juliet.

'For Jaysus sake, is that all yous can think about, her diddies? You can see feckin diddies anywhere; there's loads of them down on Sandymount Strand any day of the week.'

'Not like hers,' persisted Gurky.

'Well, at least so as yous know something about the film. The quare fellow, as you put it, is an Englishman named Laurence Harvey, and someone called Susan Shentall was Juliet.'

'Ah, I knew it,' piped up Reddy Costello, 'Me Da says all Englishmen are quare fellows.'

'Can someone tell me what a quare fellow is?' Gurky Ryan asked.

'You know that dopey bus conductor on the number 14?' answered Reddy, 'the one that puts his hand up the leg of your trousers when you're coming down the steps to get off; well, he's one.'

'How do you know?' Gurky said.

'Because he puts his feckin hand up your trousers,' explained a patient Reddy.

'And is that what quare fellows is supposed to do? Jaysus, that doesn't seem to be very much and it isn't very nice for them if they touch your mickey by accident, is it, especially if you've just done a pee?'

'Why do women have diddies?' Patsy's younger brother, Dinny, wanted to know.

'So that they can feed babies,' replied Patsy as they walked to school.

'But there's women and even girls that's got diddies that don't have babies.'

'But they have the milk in them until the babies are there.'

'But wouldn't the milk go sour if it had to wait for months or maybe years before there'd be a baby.'

'Well, I think the diddies is like a sort of fridge, it keeps the milk fresh until the baby gets it.'

'You'd imagine it'd leak a bit, wouldn't you,' said Dinny. 'When they're walking around with them full and bouncing about and all?'

'You're terrible stupid, do you know that. It's not like your mickey sticking down with the hole at the bottom ready to leak anytime. The holes in the diddies are sticking out, not down you see, and they've got them brassers to hold the diddies up and make sure the hole doesn't point down to the ground.'

'Why've we got diddies? We don't feed babies and I've never seen a hole in me diddie.'

'They're not proper diddies we've got. Anyway, Tony told me that we've got breasts; he said that's a really dirty word. Women have diddies and they call them bosoms in England, which Tony says is very posh.'

'Did you ever touch one?'

'What? Did I ever touch what?'

'A diddie, you know, a breast thing, the posh bosom thing?'

'You want to know a lot today, don't you? Did you ever hear about too much curiosity killing the shaggin cat?'

'No, but I heard Gurky Ryan talking about it in the schoolyard.'

'Gurky Ryan! What in Jesus' name would he feckin know about it?'

'He said it felt just like a bit of sponge or a piece of soft cake.'

'Will you go way out of that. You don't expect a beautiful diddie to feel like an auld bit of sponge or a piece of stale cake.'

'Gurky said soft cake not a stale bit.'

'He's talking through his shaggin hole. He doesn't know anything, I'm telling you.'

'Well, what does it feel like?'

'I don't know but it's not like those things; it's altogether different to any of those things.'

'I thought you knew; I was sure you'd felt one.'

'I have but it wasn't the same.'

'What do you mean it wasn't the same?'

'Promise first you won't say anything…promise.'

'Ok I promise.'

Patsy took a deep breath.

'Do you remember the dead house behind Marymount school, they call it the morgue?' Patsy asked.

'Yeah,' said Dinny, 'where they bring dead people when they're dead.'

'Right, well, that's where I felt one.'

'Felt one what?' Dinny asked.

'What you've been asking me you eegit, about the diddie.'

'Oh yeah. But what class of diddie would you feel in the dead house?'

'A dead one, you gobshite. What sort do you think you'd find in a dead house?'

'Was she dead then?' Dinny asked, eyes wide open.

'Yes, she was; she was a dead nun from the Poor Clares' convent.'

'I don't believe you.'

'I'm telling you, amn't I? There were several dead bodies in there but they were all old except this nun who looked lovely and young and she didn't look really dead.'

'And what? Did you have to go under all those clothes they wear, cloaks and all to get to it?'

'No, you bloody eegit. I felt it on top, just on top of the clothes. But I could still feel it.'

'That's not a real feel at all,' said Dinny, quite disgusted.

It was eight months after his sister Alana's funeral and Patsy was nearly 13. His mother depended greatly on him for help in the home. His youngest sister, Mollie, was 2 and his mother was expecting another child. Patsy would stay away from school for two to three weeks to look after the rest of the family while his mother was in hospital having her baby.

Why does she have to have so many babies? Hasn't she enough to do looking after all she has now? She's only just got over the last one and now she's having another.

Such were the boy's nagging thoughts as he set about cleaning the house following his mother's removal to hospital earlier in the day. He would go to Miss Cooney's shop and get the groceries on tick and put on the tea for his father and brother and sisters. His father's tea would be ready at 6 o'clock, always a chop or piece of ham or steak with boiled or mashed potatoes and cabbage. Or else mackerel simmered in boiling water with lots of vinegar added.

'Don't forget,' his mother had reminded him, 'your Da loves a bit of mackerel but make sure it's fresh.'

His sister, Eileen, was a great help to him. She looked after Mollie, bathing her and putting her to bed. Eileen also took her fair share of cleaning, washing and scrubbing. There was a good deal of rivalry between Patsy and his sister but an outside observer would have said they complemented each other to the benefit of themselves and everyone else who depended on them.

Eileen was thoughtful and reflective; she had a generous nature and was ever ready to help others. She also had a wistful side to her that showed itself in her frequent daydreaming of what it would be like to be somebody else, usually a film star or a famous singer.

'My friend, Gracie, told me I look like Elizabeth Taylor,' she boasted to Patsy.

'Who's she then?' Patsy asked, trying hard to annoy his sister.

'She's a film star, you thick!'

'And you look like a film star? I think Gracie needs glasses.'

'Ah, go way you. You're only interested in that auld Elvis Presley.'

'It's not me who's interested in Elvis Presley, it's Reddy Costello.'

'Yeah, well he's a right thick. He was trying to tell me that Elvis Presley has skin softer than any woman's and he doesn't even have to shave like men do cause he doesn't grow any hairs on his face. Did you ever hear anything like it?'

'Well, Reddy knows all about those things, you know; he writes off for magazines and all the stuff he can get on Elvis.'

'He's a right eegit. Do you know what he said?'

'What?'

'He said Elvis doesn't have to comb his hair, that his hair stays the same always, even when he goes to bed and gets up. Now isn't that stupid?'

'I'd say I agree with Reddy,' teased Patsy.

'Oh don't be so stupid.'

'Reddy told me,' continued Patsy, 'that Elvis doesn't even have to have his hair cut because it stays just as God made it…perfect! And Elvis doesn't have to do other things, like going to the toilet and all. And he never burps or farts or makes any noises in his stomach, and he doesn't yawn or sneeze or anything.'

'Patsy Fagan, if you believe…'

'I'm telling you Eileen, it's true.'

'You're a bigger gobshite than Reddy Costello.'

Their father expected Patsy and Eileen to look after the house and the other children when their mother was not there. He expected no less in the way his evening meal was served, simply because they were children. They had to learn to cope. And cope they did; Patsy did the cooking and took joy in putting his father's dinner on the table in front of him. He would also wash and iron his father's shirt so he would be smart and clean when he visited their mother in hospital.

'Good lad, Patsy, you're doing a grand job. I'll take you to see Rovers against Drumcondra when your Ma gets out of hospital. Would you like that now?'

'Of course I would, Da.'

'How do I look, visiting your ma?'

'You look great. That black shirt's grand. It shows up great with your sports jacket and that pink tie. Ma'll think you're going dancing.'

'Not without her I'm not, but sure we'll go to Clery's Christmas Dance when she's well again.'

Patsy was still awake in bed next to his brother, Dinny, when he heard his father opening the front door. He heard his father's footsteps on the stairs and then his whispered voice through the door.

'Are you awake, Patsy?'

'Yes, Da.'

His father's face was very close and Patsy could smell whiskey on his breath.

'What's up, Da?'

'Shush, don't wake Dinny. Your Ma had a baby boy just after midnight but the poor little creature only lasted ten minutes in this world.'

A tear from his father's eyes dropped on Patsy's lips.

'Go asleep now, son, but first say a little prayer that your Ma will be alright.'

Patsy's head sank deep into the pillow, his own tears mingling with his father's, leaving a bitter salty taste in his mouth.

Chapter 3

Patsy was going to see his brother in Killiney. Tony had "gone into service" just before his 14th birthday in a large Victorian villa on the Vico Rd. He was to learn all facets of making the Irish officer class, recently returned from India, British Colonial Africa and other parts of the British Empire, feel cared for, cosseted and important. At present, he was doing this by learning how to lay a table for breakfast in exactly the correct manner, as dictated by those who decide upon these matters. He was not a good learner but he was an excellent worker and undertook with enthusiasm any task given him.

He particularly enjoyed walking the master of the house's Irish Setters along the beach in Killiney. The owner of this beautiful villa was the leader of the Unitarian Church in Ireland and he had a special fondness for Tony. He knew he was not a good learner but, as with his houseguests, he was charmed by the youngster's eagerness to please and his willingness to go on countless errands at very high speeds, never seemingly to flag in energy.

The Unitarian rector would perhaps have taken a dim view of matters had he known that the chief attraction for his houseboy in the daily walking of the dogs on the beach, lay in a certain 14-year old's willingness to meet our young hero at a given time in the late afternoon. Deirdre was her name and her long tresses of hair perfectly matched the chestnut glistening of the Irish Setters.

'I thought you weren't allowed to work for Protestants,' said a breathless Patsy, soon after his run from Dalkey railway station to the Vico Rd.

'Don't you ever let Da hear you saying that,' answered a sage Tony.

'Yeah, but it's not only a Protestant, it's a clergyman!'

'Da says that the only true gentry in this country are the landed class which is mainly Protestant.'

'I don't think that Mr Bambrick in school would go along with Da on that,' answered an always ready-to-argue Patsy.

'Well, what does old Bambo know? I don't think he's ever been out of Dublin. He's certainly never been to England.'

'How do you know that?'

'You can tell. There's nothing posh about him at all. Just look at the lousy jackets he wears with lumps of leather on the elbows. You'd never see a teacher in England wearing anything like that.'

Tony showed his brother around the large house and Patsy was fascinated by the warren of passageways and secondary stairways that led to musty cubby holes in hidden deep regions of the house. He was mesmerised by all the military paraphernalia scattered throughout the extensive basement and cellars. They had to climb a steep stepladder to get to Tony's bedroom in the attic.

'Jesus Christ,' said Patsy, 'you wouldn't want to be drunk climbing that shaggin thing at night.'

'Come down to the big dining room and if we're lucky, we'll see England across the sea.'

They were sat in a large bay window overlooking Killiney Bay and sure enough, as visibility was almost perfect, they could make out the shapes of mountains on the far side of the Irish Sea.

'There you are,' said an excited Tony, 'those mountains are in England.'

Patsy's geography was good enough for him to know that they were seeing the Welsh mountains.

'That's Wales, not England,' he argued.

'What do you mean "Wales"? Wales is in England!'

Later, Patsy asked him how long he was going to stay working in Killiney.

'Only until Ma and Da'll let me go to England. Maybe Auntie Margie'll have me in Coventry and I'll get a job and I'll be able to pay her for me keep and send Ma home a little as well.'

'Why are you so desperate to go to England?'

'Ah, it's grand there. You've never seen anything like it. The girls wear all sorts of things you never see in Ireland. And they don't call girls "mots" the way we do. You can't imagine an English fella saying, "Oh, I'm going out with me mot tonight". He'd die of shame. They have much better names like "doll" and "bird".

'And their accents are really English. You don't hear an Englishman speaking like a big feckin culchie from Cork like you do in Ireland. I'm telling you they'd commit suicide if they spoke like that.'

They shared Tony's narrow bed that night, top to tail, as they had been used to doing at home.

'How are they taking the new baby dying?' Tony whispered.

'They're all right now, though Ma still cries a lot. Da's great though. He asks her if she wants to go to the pictures and things.'

'It got everybody going again about Alana. You'd imagine they'd get over her now seen as how it's been nearly a year.'

'I don't think they'll ever get over her,' answered Patsy, feeling annoyed.

'Well, Ma'll have more babies yet. Sure, look at Mrs Cleary; she's got eight children and she's about the same age as Ma.'

'You don't think Ma's got enough on her plate as it is?' Patsy asked.

'They don't have to have babies now, you know, if they don't want them.'

'What do you mean?'

'Well, they have these little white balloon things that the daddy puts on.'

'Puts it on what?' Patsy asked puzzled. 'What do you mean?'

'The daddy puts the balloon on his mickey to stop the stuff going into the mammy's stomach so that she doesn't have a baby.'

'I've never heard of that,' said Patsy. 'Are you sure?'

'Of course I'm sure. Your friend, Reddy, told me that when he was babysitting for his Auntie Breda, he was rooting around in his uncle's cupboard and he found two of these little balloons. He didn't know what they were for, of course, but he found out afterwards cause he took one to show to his cousin, Sheila, who knew exactly what it was.'

Patsy was feeling let down that Reddy was discussing important matters with his brother, Tony, and not even mentioning them to him, his best friend.

'Well, it's news to me, that's all I can say.'

'Reddy said they were called contradictive. But I don't know what it means,' said Tony, feeling pleased that he was clearly better informed than his younger brother who usually knew more answers than he did.

'Well, I don't know what "contradictive" means either. I wouldn't be surprised if that Reddy was making it up.'

'Oh, I think he was very serious,' answered Tony quickly, determined to prolong his feelings of superiority.

'Well, Mr Welsh told us that "contra" was a Latin word which means "against",' Patsy said, trying hard to contribute some knowledge to the issue and not to let his brother and the traitor, Reddy Costello, have it all their own way.

'I wonder,' said Tony, becoming quite excited, 'you know in England they sometimes call your mickey your "dick", which I think is a better name altogether. If "contra" means "against", do you think "contradictive" could mean "against your dick"? Like it's the enemy of your mickey to stop it giving out babies.'

'Go to sleep,' said Patsy feeling completely dejected.

Next morning, Patsy volunteered to take the dogs for their morning walk along Killiney beach. The whiteness of the sand reflected the brilliance of the early morning sun, making the boy squint in the blinding light. Both hands were busy holding the four leashes of the eager dogs that were dragging Patsy in their wake. He looked out across the blue waters towards England wondering if Tony would go there at last.

He climbed the long track to the top of Sorrento Point, so named, his father had told him, because its beauty compared well with that Sorrento near Naples. From the top, he could look back towards the city clearly seeing the twin smokestacks dwarfing the Poolbeg Lighthouse in Ringsend. To the south, he saw Bray Head, a favourite refuge for those mitching from school, and beyond Bray, the dark purples and greens of the Wicklow Mountains.

He was able to name the Little Sugar Loaf and a little to the west, its taller twin, the Great Sugar Loaf. Much higher peaks lay to the west and south and he took pride that he alone of his school friend was able to identify the different peaks and give their names.

He knew the city well and also the surrounding countryside, north to south. He had the advantage over his friends in that his father made his living in cutting down trees and digging the turf from the bogs. When dried and cured, his father sold both as fire fuels to customers he had served and nourished over many years. Patsy went with his father often to help load the lorry in the stockyard and then to deliver to the many parts of the city or the areas far beyond the city where his father had customers.

The "old gentry", his father insisted, were the best customers, and certainly the "best payers".

Throughout the year, his father organised deliveries on a carefully scheduled roster, so that he would arrive at a customer just as the turf or log shed was looking a little bare. It would be a ton or half a ton of logs or turf, carried by the sackful on his father's strong shoulders, and if there was not sufficient space in the shed for the full twenty sacks or whatever, there would always be another day to make good the shortfall provided, of course, the father remembered, which he usually did not.

His father never failed to point out and repeat the names of places and who lived where and what had happened there, and if a ghost haunted a house or church, or if an infant baby had drowned or been consumed in a fire.

'That's where an airplane full of refugee children crashed, killing all the unfortunate souls,' he explained as they drove slowly along the Enniskerry to Roundwood Road. Patsy learnt years later that the children survived.

'And over there is talk about building a war cemetery for German sailors or airmen who died somehow in Irish seas or crash landed on Irish soil,' his father would point out on every occasion they passed through Glencullen towards Powerscourt Demesne, adding in slightly sardonic voice, 'I wonder how our English neighbours across the sea will regard that.'

'That's where the IRA used to train and before them other patriots and rebels. The British built this road so they could send soldiers to capture the rebels who hid in the mountains. That's why they called it Military Road,' he said as his old lorry struggled to reach the top of the Featherbed Mountains.

'And that cross there marks the spot where the British Army shot an IRA volunteer back in 1920 when I was only six. They were the Black and Tans and just as tough as the IRA, though bad bastards they were.'

Patsy took his turn with his brothers, Tony and Dinny, to go with his father on these trips during the school holidays or on a Saturday. It would usually be a full day out and he always looked forward to the "stop for lunch" outside a butcher's shop where his father would send him for a ring of white pudding to go with the loaf of crusty hot bread and the pint of fresh creamy milk. They would have this feast in the cab of the lorry before setting off for the afternoon call. Often, they were invited into the kitchen by the housekeeper or scullery maid and were given mugs of tea or red lemonade with cake or hot scones.

It was on such a trip that Patsy became aware that the future was not the certainty that was taken for granted by his parents. He was with his father on a delivery to a fine manor house in Howth Head when he overheard him in conversation.

'But I've been coming to you over thirty years, Ma'am, ever since I was a nipper. How can you send me away now?'

'I know, Fagan, I know. It breaks my heart don't you know to have to tell you. I remember you coming with your first horse and cart, all the way out from the city and never letting us down, no matter what the weather. And then during the war, what would we have done without you? Nobody else could get enough fuel for the fire except you and you always had a few sackfuls for us.'

'Well then, Ma'am, can we not carry on in the old way?' pleaded his father.

'Haven't I told you it breaks my heart, Fagan, but Mr Hyland has decided that the fireplaces are to be closed down and a coal boiler is to be installed in the cellar that will provide hot water to the radiators for heat. I really don't understand why you can't deliver coal instead of logs and turf.'

'It's because the merchants won't let me have the coal much cheaper than they sell it to you unless I was to buy it in the hundreds of tons. I can't do that because I couldn't afford it and anyway, I haven't got a yard big enough to store hundreds of tons.'

'I'm sorry, Fagan, but there's no changing the master's opinion.'

'Oh, I'm not blaming you, Ma'am, or the master himself but the big merchants control the supply and the costs, and I don't suppose you'd want to buy coal from me for a much higher price even for old times' sake.'

'I am sorry, Fagan.'

On the way home that evening, Patsy could sense his father's anxiety, and also his fear.

Chapter 4

Gurky Ryan was in trouble, big trouble. He had arrived at school with a number of little brown paper bags each with a bar of chocolate in it, and also a box of Milk Tray chocolates that he presented to the headmaster, Mr Hayes.

'And to what do I owe this singular honour, Master Ryan?' Mr Hayes enquired.

'T'was me birthday yesterday, Sir, and me Auntie Bernie gave me a pound to spend on meself. So I just thought I'd get a few bars of chocolate for the teachers and some sweets for meself and me friends.'

'Well, your Auntie Bernie is a generous aunt indeed, and I must say that generosity must run in the family. You are to be commended, young Ryan, for a splendid display of selfless devotion to your teachers.'

At morning break and at lunchtime, teachers and pupils could be seen enjoying the sixpenny bars of Cadbury's and the headmaster was equal to Gurky's generosity in passing around the Milk Tray. Events took a turn for the worse, however, in the afternoon. Mr Hayes marched into Mr Bambrick's class accompanied by Mr Welsh and also by the parish priest, Father Fitzpatrick.

'Master Ryan' shouted Mr Hayes in front of the whole class of forty boys of 13 years of age.

'Yes, Sir,' replied Gurky Ryan, in a voice that sounded more like the quacking of a duck than of anything human.

'You told us it was your birthday yesterday and your Auntie Bernie gave you one pound to spend on yourself, did you not?'

'That's right, Sir, she did exactly that,' panted Gurky.

'Can you then explain to us, Master Ryan,' asked the headmaster, assuming what he imagined to be the stance and tone of a high court judge, 'how it comes to be that your birthday is not for another six months and that a one pound note is missing from a cardboard box in Mr Welsh's room? The box contained the money, Master Ryan, donated in pennies and sixpences and threepenny pieces by the pupils of this school for the White Fathers in Africa for their work in converting the heathens to be good Catholics and for looking after all the little black babies so they can grow up to be good Catholics as well!'

The headmaster had lost his magisterial dignity and ended his sentence in a hysterical scream.

'Disgraceful,' shouted the parish priest. 'You'll go to Hell for a sin like this, you little bowsie!'

Gurky confessed his crime and was marched away to face the music.

'Six big ones on the arse with the feckin deluxe model, not even the three-footer,' he explained to Patsy and Reddy in the yard the next day.

'And they told me Ma last night. She nearly shaggin killed me and caught me an awful blow on the head with a saucepan. I thought I was feckin dead I did. And then she had to go and borrow a pound from that cranky old whoor Mrs Burke to pay back old Hayes.'

'But why did you buy the teachers chocolate?' Reddy asked. 'I just don't understand that. I mean it's feckin stupid. You were bound to be caught.'

'"There are many things betwixt heaven and earth that are undreamt of in your philosophy" Reddy,' observed Patsy drily.

'T'was that Sister Carmel at the sodality,' answered Gurky. 'She said it didn't matter to Our Lord what bad things you did so long as you did somebody a kindness. So I thought one thing would cancel out the other. Do yous see?'

'That's what you get for listening to shaggin priests and nuns, you dozy ballocks. You're getting to be as bad as Patsy with his fuckin Shakespeare and walking all over Dublin daydreaming shite,' concluded an exasperated Reddy.

He loved walking the streets of Dublin, especially in the parts he knew well because of journeying with his father, or around the areas where he was born or had lived.

Biddy Mulligan, the pride of the Coombe; that's where I was born, in the Coombe hospital. Can't get any more Dublin than that, Da says. Ma's a culchie, born in Kildare, but not too far from Dublin. "Doesn't matter," says Da. "Culchies stick together like shite to a blanket, always get the best jobs in the civil service or in the schools. Speak the Irish you see. Keep the Dubliners out of it. Jaysus, give the Dubliners half a chance and see what sort of job they'd make of running the shaggin country."

"But you married Ma anyway whether she's a culchie or not, and you told us you used to drive the pony and trap all the way down to Kildare Town just to see her for a couple of hours. And also to see old Paddy, her da, who was also a culchie."

"Your grandfather is a gentleman and I wouldn't hear a word against him. Do you know he used to ride the bike with the solid tyres all the way from Monasterevin. He'd stop at every pub on the way. When he'd get to your great aunt Lizzie's in Churchtown, he'd be drunk and couldn't sit down with the sore arse from riding the bike. He'd go asleep in the garden and wouldn't ask you for the time of day."

"Your Ma was living with her aunt at the time and that's why aul Paddy came up on the bike. Your grandmother had died when your Ma was only a little thing and he couldn't look after the four young ones on his own so he put your Ma with her aunt to live when she was about 8. Ah, she was a grand girl, clever; you wouldn't be catching her out on the history or the reading. Sure she was a lovely slip of a girl, why shouldn't I have married her. Wasn't I lucky to get her?"

Patsy enjoyed history lessons in school especially when Mr Bambrick allowed the class to say what they thought or what their friends or relations outside of school thought about the subject matter under discussion. Ireland's history and its relationship with England was an area where opinions were readily expressed with passion.

'Robert Emmet was a great patriot who was sentenced to be hanged, drawn and quartered by the English for what they described as treason.'

'What does drawn and quartered mean, Sir?' Gurky Ryan asked.

'Having his mickey and balls cut off,' whispered Reddy Costello.

'Careful, Costello,' warned Mr Bambrick. 'It means, Ryan, pulling out the heart of the still-living victim and cutting off his arms and legs.'

'Jaysus Christ,' groaned Gurky.

'I'm glad to see Our Lord is close to your heart and lips, Ryan. As it happened, Robert Emmet was hanged and then beheaded. His heart was not torn out, nor were his limbs cut off. You must remember, boys, that all actions and behaviour must be taken in their historical context.

'That means you have to ask certain questions: did any other conquering force at the time, for example France or Spain, or any other country in the world which had occupied another country, treat the native population differently? Did the French treat the North American Indians worse or better than the English treated the Irish? How well or badly did the slave traders and American plantation owners deal with black people taken from their homes in Africa? How did the Spanish conquerors treat the Incas and Aztecs of Central and South America...You, Costello, enlighten us all now with your views.'

'Well, Sir, I don't know how them other countries treated the people living there when they came in their ships and things, but I do know one thing for certain.'

'Which is?' the schoolmaster prompted.

'The Irish weren't a bunch of shaggin savages like them Inkies and Aztecs and they weren't hanging round street corners in Africa waiting to be kidnapped. That's what me Da says they were doing and why they was easy to catch. And last of all, Sir, they weren't like the Red Indians going around with bows and arrows scalping every shaggin body they caught. So the Irish deserved to be treated better.'

'And would you say, Costello, and please watch your language, that the Romans crucified a savage when they crucified Our Lord on the cross.'

'No, Sir, but Our Lord wasn't a Catholic and He wasn't even Irish.'

Patsy stood in front of the house where he had lived until the age of 8. He stared at the dark grey walls of the 18th century Georgian house and at the familiar windows and the great hall door with its massive brass lion-head knocker which had been his hall door when he was a small child; and now through the wonder of learning history, the same hall door and the very house itself were transformed in his mind into a shrine to two young lovers who were in his eyes equal in every way to Shakespeare's young hero and heroine.

*I lived here in Emmet House, in Mount Drummond Avenue, Harold's Cross, Dublin. And **he** was here maybe in our sitting room or our bedroom, Tony's and mine. And was she here with him? Of course she was! Didn't her father throw her out for being engaged to him, for being in love with him? This is where they met! He would meet her here after his secret meetings to organise the revolt. It would be dark except for candlelight, and they could watch each other loving each other in their eyes and in their hearts.*

Did she know that he would be executed, that he could have escaped to France if he hadn't loved her so much and decided to see her one last time. Was she at his trial? Did her heart break when he spoke?

"Does the sentence of death which your unhallowed policy inflicts on my body, condemn my tongue to silence...My country was my idol! I acted as an Irishman, determined on delivering my country from the yoke of a foreign and unrelenting tyranny...Let no man dare, when I am dead, to charge me with dishonour...I am going to my cold and silent grave, my lamp of life is nearly extinguished, my race is run...I have but one request to ask at my departure from this world: it is the charity of its silence.

"Let no man write my epitaph. Let me rest in obscurity and peace, and my tomb remain uninscribed and my memory in oblivion, until other times and other men can do justice to my character. When my country takes her place among the nations of the earth, then, and not till then, let my epitaph be written. I have done."

How grand were his words and thoughts. Was she proud of him? Did you love him, Sarah Curran? Did you love him as Juliet loved Romeo: would you have died for him as he died for Ireland? He risked his life for love of you...and lost it. Of course you loved him! You were sent to Sicily to forget him and didn't his friend, Thomas Moore, write the song for you to keep forever in your heart "She is far from the Land where Her Young Hero Sleeps". But you could not live without him. You were truly his Juliet.

Chapter 5

An enlightened teacher was allowing "a weekly period for important questions".

'Do yis think aul Bambo would take it bad if I was to slip in a quick question about diddies?' Gurky Ryan asked.

'He'll give you a quick answer with the cane,' answered Patsy Fagan.

'Well, I can never think of any questions at the time and its only afterwards that I can feckin remember them, and then it's too late.'

'Why don't you get one ready before the class and keep it handy in your head till you're ready?' a helpful Patsy suggested.

'What are you telling him that for?' Reddy Costello joined in. 'Sure he hasn't got a sensible shaggin question to ask anyway. He only thinks about women and diddies and all that class of thing.'

Forty eager boys were waiting, and as soon as the last words of The Angelus were said and the Sign of the Cross was made with proper reverence, the schoolmaster allowed the first question.

'My mother says it's a disgrace that a communist country like Yugoslavia should've been allowed to send a football team to Holy Catholic Ireland and Irishmen shouldn't play football against communists. Me Da says she's talking baloney. What do you think, Sir?'

'Very good question, Browne,' answered Mr Bambrick. 'Let's open it up to the whole class. Now who's going to give a view?'

'I think his mother's an aul whoor,' whispered Reddy to his friend, Patsy, 'and I think they should stick her in the goal in Dalymount Park and let all them feckin communists fire the ball at her all shaggin night. That'll keep her feckin mouth shut.'

'What are you laughing at, Patsy Fagan?' the teacher asked. 'And you, Costello, if I hear any vulgarities from you, it'll be the deluxe model on the rear.'

'I wouldn't say any vulgarities, Sir,' protested Reddy.

'Just don't.'

'No, Sir.'

Questions were debated, argued over, and sometimes caused considerable bitterness at the moment but were also soon forgotten and harmony was restored in Mr Bambrick's class. No subject was forbidden and all points of view allowed, provided they were stated in an acceptable manner as deemed fit by the schoolmaster. Patsy learnt more about his own opinions on matters of history, literature, religion and politics by hearing the views of his classmates than all the lone introspection to which he was by nature inclined.

He listened keenly to any questions touching on Irish history and was often in some torment in trying to decide where he stood on what appeared to him to be painful issues.

'Do you think, Sir, that Ireland should have joined the war against Germany?'

'Many Irishmen went to war in British uniforms in the Royal Navy, Royal Air Force and the British Army; many thousands of them joined to fight the Nazis.'

'But the country, Sir, the government didn't declare war the way the English and Americans did. Was that right?'

'You must remember that Ireland had been free of British rule for less than twenty years when the war broke out, and the country was very weak. An awful civil war had followed British withdrawal, which many people say was the direct responsibility of the British Government. That civil war weakened the country even further and frankly, made much of the population little inclined to fight on the same side as England. But do please remember many thousands of Irish fought in the war and many died. What do you other boys think?'

'My uncle Tom said that De Valera should never have said he was sorry that Hitler was dead,' shouted one boy.

'Is it not right,' answered Mr Bambrick, 'that a Christian should feel sad at anyone's death no matter how many sins they have committed?'

'Me Da went to Birmingham to work in the factory in the war and was nearly blown up by them German planes,' called another boy.

'And my Da and me Ma also, both of them. That's where they met in the factory in somewhere called Bolton, making bits for tanks.'

'That's nothing, for Jaysus sake. My uncle Eamon was in the air force flying with the pathfinders and everybody was firing at his plane from the ground. He got a decoration from the King of England…the Queen's aul fella.'

'What's an Irishman getting a decoration from the feckin king of England? Is he a traitor or what?'

'Watch your shaggin mouth.'

'Sure, I was only joking.'

'Was there rationing in Dublin during the war, Sir?'

'Of course there was. People couldn't get petrol unless you had special coupons and there were shortages of food and tea and coffee, all the sorts of stuff that has to be imported into the country.'

'Was it as bad here as it was in England?'

'No, I don't think so. But then I don't suppose it was as bad in England as it was in Germany or in France.'

'But it was the Germans who started it, wasn't it? They deserved to suffer didn't they, Sir?'

'Would you say that was true for the babies who were born in Germany during the years of the war and had no responsibility for the war at all?'

'They shouldn't be having babies when they start a shaggin war,' chimed in Reddy Costello.

'Thank you for your special insight, Costello. What would we do without your wisdom?'

'I don't know, Sir.'

'But even if our government didn't declare war on Germany, they must've wanted one side to win more than the other,' asked another enquiring voice. 'amn't I right, Sir?'

'T'was England, you eegit,' shouted Gurky Ryan.

'No t'wasn't, it was America we wanted to win.'

'But wasn't America and England fighting on the same side?'

'And the Russians as well.'

'Me Ma says the Russians are godless communists and should have been invaded by us when the Nazis were killed.'

'That shaggin Browne and his Ma again,' Reddy whispered into Patsy's ear. 'And who does she mean by "us"?'

'Did any bombs drop on Dublin, Sir?'

'Well, yes, there were one or two bombing incidents in 1941 in Dublin and along the east coast. Around thirty people were killed. Strangely, a bomb destroyed part of a Jewish synagogue in Dublin.'

'You didn't answer the question, Sir.'

'Sorry…the question?'

'Which side were we on?'

'Well, as we've heard today, many of us know of Irishmen and women who fought in the armed forces of Britain or who worked in factories in England. Now is there anyone who knows of anybody Irish who fought in the German forces?'

'What about Lord Ha-y-Ha? Me Da says he was Irish.'

'You'd better ask your Da then because I don't know too much about him eh, Lord Haw-Haw, I think, but thank you for the question,' answered a tiring and increasingly impatient Mr Bambrick. 'Now then, last question please?'

'Sir, is it true that people were queuing up in Dublin in 1944 and 1945 to go and see Bing Crosby pictures while at the same time the Nazis were killing thousands of Jews?' Patsy Fagan asked.

'Yes, Fagan, that's correct but so were people in New York and Washington, and young people were dancing and getting out of life what they could in London and Glasgow. And no doubt in liberated Paris, they were drinking wine and going to clubs to listen to Edith Piaff singing. What the Germans were doing to the Jews was not the fault of the Irish and you shouldn't feel guilty about it.

'What they did is too big a crime for any one nation to shoulder, even Germany itself. Only the whole Earth can bear such a burden. I hope that answers your question.'

In the following weeks, Patsy read everything he could find about the Second World War and what had happened to the Jews. He also read keenly about Irish rebellions and their leaders and would stop on streets and at buildings in Dublin where fighting had taken place or uprisings had begun.

He asked his mother about the Jews who had been murdered in the war and was surprised to learn that their own landlord, when they had lived in Emmet House, was a Jew who had left Germany in the early thirties to escape the coming persecution.

'What, and he owned Emmet House?'

'Yes,' answered his mother, 'and we rented the top of the house. He was a very kind and gentle man, Mr Marcus, who charged a very fair rent. He was always asking your Da to buy the house.'

'Why?'

'Mainly because of the amount of damage you, Tony and Dinny were always doing. You had the poor man's heart broken with all the repairs he had to be always doing. You were little devils, I'm telling you.'

'And why didn't Da buy the house, Ma? It would've been great to own the house where Robert Emmet was arrested.'

'It would've been far better if the poor man hadn't been arrested at all. Your Da wanted a house for ourselves on our own, and there were other people living in Emmet House, other tenants. And haven't we got a lovely house here?'

Patsy and Dinny were going on a visit to their old house. Patsy had asked his sister, Eileen, if she had wanted to go with them.

'I'm not interested in that aul Robert Emmet history,' Eileen said, 'that you keep on about. Jesus, you'd think you had enough of that at school without wanting it on a Saturday as well.'

'It's not just about him but also Mr Marcus and the Jews.'

'I don't want to spend me time talking about the Jews. Anyway, Sister Angelica told us that the Jews were to blame for Our Lord's death on the cross; and she said the Jews could've got the aul Romans to let him go free, but instead, they were so jealous because he could do the miracles and all and they thought Our Lord was more powerful than them, and so they got the Romans to let out this other aul thief—Barabar or something like that—and so Our Lord got crucified.'

'So you don't want to go?'

'No, I don't, Patsy Fagan. I'm going to The Princess to see *Rock Around the Clock with Bill Haley and The Comets*.'

'For Jaysus' sake, how many times have you seen that picture?'

They walked past their own little cowboys and Indians canyon known in their neighbourhood as "The Glen". It had a small stream running through it and was steeply banked with grassy slopes with an abundance of ash, lime and beech trees. Hawthorn and blackberry bushes provided perfect ambush cover for the competing young gangs of boys who fought weekly battles for the precious territory.

Those shot from week to week with Colt 44 pistols and Springfield rifles, or those who simply were shot with arrows or impaled on long lances were always fully recovered in time for the next decisive encounter. Leadership of the gangs usually depended on who was sporting the newest toy revolver or who had fashioned the best bow or spear.

When not engaged in battle, the boys spent a good deal of time in throwing stones at the large population of water rats which inhabited the stream or in trying to ensnare rabbits with pieces of string and wire. Their paradise was being slowly eroded by the plans of the landowner to fill his small glen by allowing it to be used as a refuse tip by local residents. When filled and rolled and flattened, the land would be used for house building.

Patsy and Dinny walked along the footpath overlooking the River Dodder seeing who was first to spot a trout or roach or rudd. They stopped at the Orwell Bridge and looked over the parapet of the bridge at the dark deep waters below.

'Do you think you'll ever be able to do it?' Dinny asked.

'Of course I will,' answered Patsy.

'When, when will you?'

'I don't know, stupid, do I? When I'm older. Maybe next summer.'

Both boys envied the brave lads who climbed over the parapet and stood on the narrow ledge before diving or jumping to the water eight feet below.

'Tony's been doing it for a long time now,' said Dinny.

'Yeah, but he's older than me,' Patsy protested.

'Not that much, only a bit over a year.'

'But a year is miles more,' said Patsy wanting this conversation to end.

'Anyway, I'm not interested in doing stupid things like that anymore.'

'Y'are,' insisted Dinny. 'You're just scared to do it and you're jealous that Tony can do it and you can't. And he's the only one who can climb that big fir tree in Landscape Avenue and you can't.'

'Don't be such an eegit. I can climb that fir tree anytime.'

'No, you can't, cause I've seen you trying but you can only get to the first big branch and then you give up and come down.'

'Well, I'll show you tomorrow if I can't, you'll see.'

'Bet you don't. And bet you're jealous of Tony.'

'C'mon for crying out loud or we'll never get to shaggin Harold's Cross,' said a much put out Patsy.

Mrs McNamara opened the great hall door and studied the two boys quizzically before recognition dawned.

'Ah hello, Patsy Fagan, and it's yourself, Dinny…come in out of that and let me see yous. Sure, I haven't seen yous for ages. Yous never feckin come near me at all now. I only saw your Ma in Camden Street about two weeks ago and I was saying to her that yous should come and see me. Would yous like some lemonade?'

'Yes please, Mrs Mac,' answered Patsy.

'What about you, Dinny?'

Dinny had not seen Mrs McNamara for more than two years and it seemed to him that he was looking at a very old woman that he did not know. He was hiding himself a little behind the end of a Victorian sofa, feeling strangely shy.

'Come on, Dinny darling, would you like some or would you rather some milk?'

'Answer Mrs Mac,' pleaded Patsy.

'Do you not remember me, Dinny?'

'No.'

'Sure, I looked after you when you were a baby and many is the time that your Ma brought you down and put you on that sofa when she had to go out to do the shopping and the weather was too bad to take you with her. Come over here now and let me see you and you can ask me all about meself.'

As he sat by her drinking his lemonade, he allowed her to pet him and ruffle his hair, and he lost his initial shyness.

'Are you very old?' he asked her.

'Dinny,' warned Patsy, don't be bold or I'll tell Ma.'

'Shush, Patsy, don't tell your Ma anything. Sure he's not being rude. He just wants to know the things that are important to himself. I'm 73, Dinny, so there, what do you think of that. I can remember seeing Queen Victoria when I was a little girl.'

Patsy was looking at the room as if he had never seen it before. He was seeing the photographs, drawings and prints in the room through new eyes. He had been in this room many times before but now it had great possible connections with his new heroes and a direct link with the Jews in Nazi Germany.

Why does she smell like the broken biscuits in Miss Cooney's shop? It's a sweet smell like when Ma is mixing all the stuff for the Christmas cake. Why's she letting him ask all those questions? Would she know if Robert Emmet was ever in this room? Does she know that Mr Marcus is a Jew and that he came from Germany?

Of course you feckin eegit. Wasn't she living here long before Ma and Da? And doesn't Mr Marcus still own the house? I wonder what she thinks of the

Jews and how they were killed in the war. She can remember Queen Victoria. Lots of the houses Da goes to have pictures of Queen Victoria on the walls and also of King George V and Queen Mary. "The old king and queen," Da calls them.

'What are all those brown lines on your face?' Dinny was asking.

'Dinny, I've told you,' shouted Patsy.

'Leave him be,' said Mrs McNamara. 'We're getting on like a house on fire, aren't we, Dinny? Those are wrinkles. You get them when you're old.'

'I've never seen them on old people. Grandad hasn't got them like that.'

'No but your granny, your da's mother has them, hasn't she? It's just that my skin is a little dark and the wrinkles show up that much more.'

'Do they hurt you?'

'No, not at all.'

'Can I touch them?'

'Yes, of course you can. There, can you reach me face now?'

'They're soft,' said Dinny. 'I thought they'd be hard and a bit crackly.'

'Well, now isn't that a nice surprise for you. Did you know that your brother, Patsy, also had marks on his face, now all completely disappeared, thank God.'

'No, what was that?'

'Well, I'm sure Patsy won't mind me telling you, do you, Patsy? And it's also a warning to you not to do dangerous things. It was when Patsy was about 7 and all the boys were in the garden playing around a big bonfire that Mr Starkey from upstairs, God rest his soul poor man, had lit to burn all the rubbish. Didn't that Andrew Glynn from Drummond Place pick up a burning bicycle tyre with a stick and start to twirl it around and around, and the flames were coming out of it, and the tyre flew off the stick and wrapped itself around poor Patsy's face.'

I smelt me hair burning and felt me skin boiling. Somebody grabbed me and knocked me to the ground and rubbed grass and weeds and dirt into me face. They pulled off the tyre but I felt bits of melting rubber stick to me.

"Like a sacrificial lamb given up as an offering," the doctor said. "Best black doctor in Dublin", according to Da, "only black doctor in the city". Endless visits to the hospital and to his surgery. Dr Peglow from the Gold Coast

in Africa. "How is the burnt offering?" Hoc est enim Corpus meum. *Given up for you.*

Creams, oils, ointments and salves spread and rubbed into me tender skin and flesh. Blue and violet bottles poured onto me scalp down to me throat by the pint, and slowly the healing wins through and I'm back to me old ways. When I look closely, I can still see the lines in me face that were made by the steel wire in the rim of the tyre.

'How is Mr Marcus?' Patsy asked.

'Ah, he's grand,' Mrs Mac answered. 'He's a lovely man altogether. It's an awful tragedy his wife dying last year, God rest her poor soul. After all, they'd been through, getting out of Germany and making a new life in Dublin and all.'

'Does he still come every week?'

'Of course he does. Only now he's not afraid to come like he used to be. My Jesus, yous gave him an awful time, you and Tony, and even you, Dinny, although you were only 2 or 3. Yous were always up to devilment and smashing things. Poor aul Mr Marcus would wait for your Da and roar up the stairs after him. "Mista Fagan, Mista Fagan, can you kommen down here please; can you see the damage your boys done? They have my heart broken, Mista Fagan."

"They broke the lavatory pot again. The vorst is Tony and he is oldest, and then is the Patsy and now even the young baby Dinny. And what you think? They bring that dirty arse Gurky Ryan and he shiten in my lavatory. Why not he shiten in his own house? No, he come here with his comrades and after he shiten in my bowl, he takes the stones from the garden and throw them in the lavatory and do the breaking. It is three times this year."

"They try to make the vater in the bowl flood over the top to come onto the floor but they put big stones into the pot and break it again. Mr Fagan, why not you buy this beautiful old house. I sell it to you at a wery cheap price for one thousand pounds. What you think? Say yes, please, Mista Fagan." I can hear the poor man now, God love him, and your father would come down, and Jesus, the language out of him.

'He'd give yous a right hiding over his knee with those big hands, and the screams and roars out of yous, and Mr Marcus shouting at him, "That's right, Mista Fagan, give their arses a good scalping and catch that Gurky Ryan and do same for the little shagger". But Gurky was off, you wouldn't catch that little gurrier till the sun went down over Alaska.'

Patsy was disappointed when Mrs McNamara admitted to knowing little about Robert Emmet and bewildered that she did not share his astonishment that she lived in a house which was the very one in which he was arrested. She had told Patsy that she was more interested in a good picture like, *The Bells of St Mary's*, or listening to a good story on the radio, "so long as it has a happy ending". She was not able to help him much either in the matter of the Jews in Germany despite her acquaintance with Mr Marcus.

He was determined he would pursue his interest in both matters whenever the opportunity arose. New excitements were afoot, however, to distract even the most ardent of devotees, whatever the cause.

'Did you hear it? Did you hear it on the wireless?'

'What? Did I hear what?'

'The sputnik, you shaggin amadan,' screamed Reddy Costello.

'Yeah, we were listening all last night on Radio Eireann. Wasn't it great?'

'Me aul man said it's the end of the world,' added Gurky Ryan.

'Thank Jaysus there isn't many like your aul fella,' replied Reddy.

'Dinny and me are going to Roberts' radio shop this evening. The fella who works there has a radio receiver that can pick up the sputnik signals clear as anything, and he's asked all the people in Landscape Avenue to go down tonight and listen. They even had an announcement about it on Radio Eireann,' said Patsy, knowingly making his friends jealous.

'You don't listen to that shaggin Radio Eireann, do you?' An envious Reddy asked. 'That's only shite that radio station. Me Da says only the mentally retarded and culchies listen to it.'

'There's nothing wrong with it,' protested Patsy. 'You get good bits on history and sometimes there's good plays and songs.'

'Good songs!' Reddy exclaimed. 'All you get is shaggin advertisements about feeding pigs and clearing up horseshit. And the one for Walton's pianos that really kills me: "If you sing a song, do sing an Irish song...Land of song said the warrior bard", sung by some drunken aul whoor of a ballocks. What the fuck would Elvis say if he heard that shite? He'd never come to this country, I'm telling you.'

'I like Irish songs,' said Gurky Ryan.

'Feck off you,' answered Reddy Costello.

And with the rest of the world, Patsy and his family and Reddy and Gurky Ryan listened to the beep of the Soviet satellite, and in the still long evenings of autumn, Dubliners went into the streets and into their gardens to watch the small metal ball trace its bright path across the Irish sky. The space age had arrived.

'Do you think, Sir, there's life on Mars?' Patsy asked, in Mr Bambrick's "question time".

'There may be life elsewhere in the universe but I don't think we'll find any little green men on Mars,' answered Mr Bambrick.

'Jet Morgan and Journey into Space was me favourite programme,' chimed in Gurky Ryan. 'They were always finding Martians and Moonmen everywhere in space. If Jet Morgan found them, there's bound to be dozens all over the place.'

'They weren't real in Journey into Space,' said Reddy. 'They was just made that up for the story.'

'I know that,' answered Gurky. 'But the man who made up the stories must've got the idea from something and that could've been true.'

'If they found people living on other planets, Sir,' asked Patsy, 'would that mean there's no God?'

'Why would it mean there's no God, Fagan?' the schoolteacher answered.

'Well, Jesus is God and He came to the earth to save us. And He was born as one of us and lived in Jerusalem and around there. If there were people on other planets, would He be their God as well?'

'Of course He would, you eegit,' said Reddy Costello. 'There's only one God who made the whole universe, isn't there? He's the Catholic God.'

'So there'd have to be Catholics on Mars.'

'Would there be Irish living on Mars and all?' Gurky Ryan asked.

'And Protestants?'

'And Pagans?'

'And Communists?'

'And Jews?

And Americans?'

'And Queers?'

'And Elvis?'

'Now listen, boys, we want a serious debate and not a lot of rowdy comments. Patsy Fagan asked a serious question and he deserves a serious answer. The human race has always been presented as the centre of God's universe; next to the angels, mankind has been seen as God's most important creation.'

'If at some time in the future, we discover life elsewhere, especially intelligent life, one of the first questions we would want to ask would be if they knew about God.'

'And supposing they didn't,' Patsy said, 'supposing they knew nothing about God or Jesus or Mary or anything like that?'

'Well, what conclusion would you come to?' Mr Bambrick asked.

'I'd say that God was only on the Earth, and that means He can't have created the whole universe. He'd only be a God for us and that wouldn't be right.'

'There's no feckin people out there anyway,' Reddy Costello called out. 'And if there was, they'd only be like the frogs and insects and things and they wouldn't have any brains so they wouldn't have a God anyway, so it doesn't make any difference.'

A little later in the year, the Soviets sent another satellite into space, this time carrying a dog, an event which gave great satisfaction to Reddy Costello who proclaimed loudly:

'There, I told yous all, there's only animals in space!'

Chapter 6

Patsy was on his way into the city to buy parts for a telescope he planned to make from a pattern he had cut out of a magazine. Ever since sputnik, he had read and collected everything he could find on space exploration, the planets and the stars. He had visited the observatory at Dunsink and had been thrilled to look through the lens of the great telescope at the planet Jupiter.

Although, anxious to reach the centre of the city, he got off the bus at Leonards' Corner so that he could walk down Clanbrassil St and look in all the old shops as he made his way towards St Patrick's and Christ Church cathedrals.

It always hits you, the smell of the knackers' yard. Turning dead horses into glue. What bits of the horse do they use? Must be the bones or the hooves; they couldn't use the flesh or the skin, could they? Terrible smell. Seems to go up your nose and down into your stomach. There's much nicer smells in Dublin. Hops and porter from the brewery when you get down as far as High St.

There's Granny's pub, "The Bunch of Grapes". She has a bottle of Guinness in there every day. "That's what keeps her going," Auntie Peggy says. "She wouldn't manage without it, I'm telling you." It's supposed to be good for you. I can't stand the taste of the stuff myself, bitter and thick like cough mixture. Granny and granda live up there in Harty Place. Should I go and see them? No, I'll leave them in peace. I'll call another time.

Funny really, granda's never seen me. Blinded in the war, the First World War that is, the one they call the Great War; I don't see how any war can be great. Anyway, not when they kill all those people and those Jewish women and children. Concentration camps. Where they put the Jews and gypsies as well, and even some Catholics. Mr Bambrick told us the British invented concentration camps. I don't believe that.

Granda feels me on the face with his hands to see who I am. "Ah, there y'are, Patsy, how're you and how's your ma?" Funny the way he's always saying "Yes,

I see, I see", when he can't see. Wonder why they always wear black clothes? Granny—black dress, black stockings, black cardigan, black coat, black hat. And granda—black jacket, black trousers, black waistcoat. They're not in mourning or anything.

His eyes look like those white marbles, not the glass ones, the white ones with the cloudy bits and little blue streaks. And he holds his head to one side like he's trying to see with his ear. "Patsy, will you go and get five Woodbines from Kelly's, there's a good lad. And make sure he gives you the right change."

They trained him to make baskets out of dried reeds when he came home from the war in 1919. Da said it would've broken his heart if he'd seen the state of Dublin after the fighting and the firing on the General Post Office. O'Connell St was destroyed. "They made Hill 16 in Croke Park out of the rubble," Da said.

He had a job in the cellar of a pub called "The Old Grinding Young"—queer name for a pub—washing the bottles. He took off his trousers and got into a big steel vat wearing his long johns and felt around for the bottles, and washed them and then reached out for the wire basket on the edge of the vat, and put them in there.

"I could do that you see even though I was blind, cause all I had to do was feel for everything." I don't think I'd like to drink beer from those particular bottles, not if I could help it. Funny though he didn't smell of beer. He had more of a pissy smell off him, not really bad though.

'In Nomine patris, et Filii, et Spiritus Sancti. Amen.'

The Fagans were at Midnight Mass on Christmas Eve in the Church of the Good Shepherd, in Churchtown. It was a newly built church and members of the Catholic hierarchy had come to join in the holy celebrations with the parish priest and the other local clergy who felt very honoured by the attention their suburban parish was receiving from the Archdiocese of Dublin. The archbishop would explain early in the New Year how much the new parish would be expected to pay into the archdiocesan coffers.

'*Introibo ad altare Dei,*' chanted the auxiliary bishop.

'*Ad Deum qui laetificat juventutem meam,*' responded at least twenty altar boys.

'Do you know how to remember that line?' Patsy whispered to his brother, Dinny.

'No, how?'

'Just say, "A dame stole a pussycat, a Jew man got the blame".'

'Shush yous two,' said their mother, who was again in the later stages of pregnancy.

Patsy loved the whole pageant of a sung High Mass. It was for him theatre on a grand scale, a great tangle of colour and light, of music and words, of movement and stillness, of sound and silence.

It's like the altar boys are the pawns on a chessboard. Not really important and lots of them. Who's the king? The bishop of course! There's no queen in this game. No, you're wrong. It's the Queen of Heaven, she's up there on the wall, the big statue. She's not on the board though, must've been captured somehow. What about the bishop? The chess bishop I mean, not the real bishop. Jesus, this is getting feckin confusing.

Don't curse at Mass. There's the bishop, the fella who carries the big cross at the head of the procession. Right, now who are the knights? What about your man with the thurible, censer some people call it, swinging it backwards and forwards like a madman, likely to hit somebody on the head. And the castles? The two gobshites with the bells and the incense-boat carrier.

Concentrate now on the Mass and pray for Alana. Why? She never committed any sins. Pray for Ma that she'll be all right with the new baby, and Tony, that he'll be OK in England. "Godless country," Noel Browne's mother calls it. "Bigoted aul cow," me Da calls her. I wonder if Robert Emmet is still in purgatory. Or other patriots who died for Ireland?

Hard to imagine Patrick Pearse sitting about in Purgatory waiting to go to Heaven. I'll pray for them as well and also Sarsfield and Parnell and Michael Collins, and me little baby brother, James, who died after only ten minutes and who we never knew. Looking forward to something to eat, fasting all day to receive Holy Communion. Can't help the noises in me belly. Mustn't touch the host with your teeth or it'll be a mortal sin.

"Keep your teeth well away from Our Saviour's body in the form of the communion bread," Sister Agnes always warned us. "This is the real living body of Jesus and it's a mortal sin for anyone to put their teeth into Our Blessed Lord. If I see anyone touching His Sacred Body with their dirty teeth, I'll have no mercy on them at all. I'll peel the skin off them with the stick."

I hated her; still do. Shush, you can't hate people at Mass. Remember when you made your First Holy Communion?

Jaysus, it was gas. Going around all the aunties and uncles getting money and things. You were only 7 so you didn't feel embarrassed or anything. Jeeze, can you imagine it now? You'd be mortified, all that waiting for the money like beggars. You didn't know if the coins were pennies or half-crowns, or maybe a few two-bob bits. Sneak a look at your hand and try not to show your disappointment.

Half the kids in Dublin doing the rounds of the relations. Still, they all tried to be generous and give you a nice warm welcome. Auntie Masie at her door, smelling of rashers and cigarettes. "Well would yis look at Patsy Fagan. Ah, Jayney Mac, isn't he gorgeous? Com'ere, Patsy, and give us a hug. There's something for your First Holy Communion." And the coins would be slid into your hand or pocket.

Of course, I had to go to me first confession before the First Holy Communion. Sister Agnes had got us ready to go into the confession box. "Don't leave any of your sins out. Remember to tell the priest everything you've done wrong. All your bad language and lies, and when you've stolen things, no matter how small, and any dirty thoughts that you've had. And don't forget Our Lord knows everything, and if you try to fool him and not tell all your sins through the priest, that's a very serious sin itself and you won't be easily forgiven. Don't forget if you die in a state of mortal sin, you'll go straight to hell!"

"Bless me Father for I have sinned, this is my first confession."

"Yes, my son, tell me everything," the priest said in his big culchie accent. "I told me Ma lies and I stole biscuits from the tin, and I blamed that on me brother, Tony, and Ma gave him a good clout for that. And I didn't say me prayers even though me Da told me to."

"Yes, my son, anything else?"

"Well, yes, there's something…"

"Not dirty thoughts I hope."

"Me ma's always telling me not to get dirty but I always forget and I do get dirty, and I fell in the canal and I got scruffy dirty, but I'm going to get better."

"Alright then, alright. Was that it then?"

'Well, no, it was…'

"What?"

"Well, you know the deadhouse at Marymount, the one they call the mortally?"

"You mean the mortuary. Yes, what about it?"

"Sometimes they've pennies or even half-crowns on the eyes of the dead people."

"Yes, what about them?"

"Me brother, Tony, and me went in there and we took all the money off the eyes and went to Sweeney's shop and spent it all on sweets."

"My Sweet Jesus Christ Almighty, you stole pennies from the dead?"

"Yes, Father."

"Soldiers of Christ," Mr Welsh told us, "that's what confirmation is all about."

We didn't have Sister Agnes for our confirmation because I was 10 and at Milltown. Mr Welsh got us ready and tested us on all the catechism questions and the prayers we had to know.

"I don't want any of you to let me down when the archbishop comes and asks you your question. Just give him a clear answer as well as the name you've chosen to be a soldier of Christ."

The archbishop came to the church in Milltown and it was packed with our parents and all. Tony and me were making our confirmation together though he was a year older than me. The archbishop said we were very lucky to be confirmed in a special year dedicated to Our Lady.

"The Holy Father in Rome has named this year Marian Year. You boys and girls are not only Soldiers of Christ but also special guards of Mary, Our Mother."

"Why doesn't he call it Mary Year instead of Marian Year if it's all about Our Lady?" Gurky whispered to me when we were in the church.

"It's the same thing, you eegit."

"No, it's not. I've a cousin called Marian and she's not Mary cause Mary is my other cousin."

Gurky said the archbishop was a bit thick. *"He asked me to tell him what was meant by the Blessed Trinity, and I explained to him that I couldn't because it was a mystery. And he said yes but could I tell him what it was all about. But I had to tell him again that I couldn't because it was a mystery and nobody understands about mysteries or else they wouldn't be mysteries, and I thought he knew that being an archbishop.*

"And then, I couldn't believe it but he asked again saying I was just to tell him what the Blessed Trinity means for us Catholics and I didn't need to try and explain the teeology or something like that. Well, I was really annoyed and lost

me rag. So, I told him to wash out his feckin ears as I wasn't going to tell him again that it was a shaggin mystery so I couldn't tell him what it means to Catholics or anybody else for that shaggin matter. And he said I wasn't to be cheeky and he was going to tell aul Hayes so I'd get six of the best. Jaysus, I wasn't been shaggin cheeky."

Chapter 7

Christmas morning and Tom Fagan, as he did every morning, brought his wife, Nuala, a cup of tea in bed. He lit the fire in the sitting room using newspaper, kindling sticks and turf. It was the turf he himself had cut in the early spring up in the Dublin Mountains. He worried how long the same turf cuttings and his supply of timber would continue to provide him with a living. Everywhere his customers were turning to coal and in recent times, he had found it difficult to make a decent wage.

Occasional shortages of domestic coal allowed him the opportunity to jump in and sell a few tons of logs or turf. But he knew he could not depend on such chance to look after his young and growing family. His mind had been mulling over some suggestions that a friend had made to him about the possibility of using his capital to buy a small garage and go into motorcar sales. He was uneasy about the venture but could not see any other possibilities.

Movement upstairs, however, soon distracted him and he began the much-enjoyed job of cooking sausages, rashers, black and white pudding, tomatoes, eggs and fried bread. By the time Patsy and Eileen had come down to lay the table, he had made the big teapot of tea, now wetting on a low flame on the gas cooker. He was slicing a large fresh turnover that Downes, the bakers, had delivered the day before.

He gave Eileen the job of spreading the softened butter ('A good thick spread now, Eileen.'). Dinny arrived making as much noise as possible, clattering door against chair and then scraping the chair legs along the linoleum-covered floor.

'Will you stop doing that, you noisy little get,' his father ordered.

'Can I open me presents now?'

'No, you can't. You'll wait like everybody else until you've had your breakfast.'

'I'm not hungry, Da. I don't want any breakfast.'

'OK then, you can sit there by the fire and shaggin starve until we've had our breakfast, but you're not going near those presents.'

'Ah, Da!'

'You can ah Da all you feckin want. Now do you want your breakfast?'

'Yeah, OK.'

'Don't do us any favours and say shaggin "please". Now get up off your arse and go and check the fire in the living room and then come back here for your grub. Eileen, go upstairs and see does your Ma want a hand and tell her breakfast is on the table.'

'Can I put some records on, Da?' Patsy asked.

'No, son, put on the radio, the BBC Light Programme. There's bound to be some good carols and songs.'

'I'll bet you're hoping that that aul Bing Crosby will be on there again with his White Christmas,' said Eileen, coming back down the stairs, adding, 'Ma'll be down in a minute.'

'I suppose you'd rather have that screaming Elvis Presley,' answered her father. 'Sure that yoke can't sing a note. If he stood behind a newspaper, you wouldn't hear him. What would he do without a microphone stuck down his gob for Christ's sake?'

'Let's have no blasphemy in this house on Christmas Day,' Nuala Fagan said, coming into her kitchen with her two hands resting on her swollen belly.

'Give your mother a chair, Patsy. Are you ready for another cup of tea, Child?' her husband asked, calling her by his most sufferingly patient pet name.

'I am but I just want to be telling yous all that we're turning over to Radio Eireann for the sung Mass from High St Church at 11 o'clock.'

'Jaysus,' groaned Dinny. 'We went to Midnight Mass last night; that's what you get when you have a culchie for a ma.'

'What did you say?' Nuala demanded.

'Nothing Ma.'

'That's what I can expect when your Da doesn't know how to respect the real gentry of this country. The so-called culchies have been looking after all you Dublin jackeens for years. I don't know what yous would do without us to teach in your schools, and doctor yous when you're sick, and nurse yous when you're in hospital and...'

'And make you a nice cup of tea every morning in bed and be a right pain in the arse,' Tom Fagan said with affection.

The morning was full of excitement and the air bursting with the wild yelps and screams of delight as presents from parents and grandparents were opened. Some presents did not survive intact for more than a few minutes as their ability to withstand great pressure from pulling, pushing, stretching and squeezing was fully tested. Alas, some were not able for the demands made of them and succumbed into oblivion. Patience, tolerance, nerves and temper were equally tried and became more frayed as this Christmas Day wore on.

'Time we were setting the table for Christmas dinner,' announced Nuala in the late afternoon.

'Yeah! Yeah!' Sitting Bull and Crazy Horse whooped, wearing full war party head-dress of the Sioux and Apache tribes, bought by their granny in Camden St.

'Can I light the Christmas candle on the table, Ma?' Patsy asked.

'Can I do it as well, Ma?' Dinny screamed.

'Yes, but for goodness sake be quiet. Now let's get everything ready. Your da'll be in shortly.'

Patsy rolled up a piece of old newspaper to serve as a candle taper and lit it from the sitting room fire. Dinny likewise rolled his paper and took his light from Patsy's flame and then rushed to be the first to light the Christmas candle. Patsy elbowed him aside and reached across the table with his now considerable flame.

Nobody quite knew how it happened but Dinny's and Patsy's shouts and cries brought their mother and sister rushing into the dining room where they saw two Red Indian war bonnets going up in flames, and the paper chains and paper balls that formed the better part of the Christmas decorations, attached to the dining room ceiling, had also been set on fire as burning war bonnets had somehow touched them.

Nuala and Eileen reacted quickly. Nuala took a basin of washing-up water from the sink and threw it over the heads of her two sons and Eileen took a broom to the remainder of the ceiling decorations and swept them to the floor.

'What in Jaysus Christ's name is going on?' Tom Fagan asked, as he walked in the door having spent the last two hours in Lalor's public house by Harold's Cross Bridge, quite illegally of course on Christmas Day.

No serious harm was done and nothing more than singed hair and eyebrows suffered by the two sorry-looking Native American warriors. The scorched and sodden head-dresses were dumped into the dustbin and the debris from the burnt decorations in the dining room soon disappeared through the efforts of Nuala and Eileen. Tom Fagan held his peace and was quickly directed to the carving of turkey, ham and beef.

'We have a letter from your brother, Tony, to read,' Nuala announced. 'It arrived the day before yesterday but we thought it'd be nice to read it to yous today at dinner.'

'Lucky the shaggin thing didn't go up in flames as well,' said Tom.

'Language, Tom, please.'

'C'mon, Ma, read it,' Eileen pleaded. 'I bet he's having a great time, lucky beggar.'

'You're not doing too bad yourself, me girl,' her father joked. 'I've noticed that ginger Reddy Costello giving you the eye.'

'Oh, Da, Holy Mary! Not that awful eegit. He's gawky and has that terrible colour hair. I'd die if I was seen with him. And he's always got snot hanging from his nose.'

'Eileen, please,' cried her mother. 'We're at dinner. Tom, stop teasing her.'

'I'll tell Reddy what you said and you can be sure he won't be looking at you again,' said Patsy.

'You can tell him anything you like cause I won't be looking at him or his aul Elvis Presley.'

'Are we going to hear Tony's letter or not?' their father demanded.

'Are you giving us a choice?' Dinny risked.

'Ok,' Nuala began, 'here it is:

"Dear Ma, Da, Patsy, Eileen, Dinny, Mollie, and the new baby if it's born, I hope yous are all well and having a good Christmas. Over here they spell it 'Xmas' everywhere. I only saw that once or twice in Dublin but everything here is really modern. Auntie Margie sends her love and all to everybody and Uncle Dinny says the same for him.

"I went with Uncle Dinny to his working men's club in Tilehill which is a place in Coventry on Saturday night. It was really great. You should see all the Teds there with their drainpipes and long jackets and they wear the skinny ties. There was a band there and the singer was like Tommy Steele, really cool. I'm hoping that I'll be able to go and see the real Tommy Steele and also Marty Wilde when they come to Coventry.

"The people at the working men's club call me Paddy. They call all Irish people Paddy, which I suppose is handy for them because then they don't have to remember your name or anything. But if you are not looking at them when they are talking, then you don't know which Paddy they mean if there is more than one.

"Uncle Dinny says that the job he got me at the Sunbeam factory is really good and I'll be able to make something of meself. I'm paying Auntie Margie fifteen bob a week. I wish I could send yous home some money but I'm not earning enough yet. Auntie Margie says you will understand and that when I'm earning more, I'll be able to send yous home some more. We are having turkey on Christmas [sorry Xmas] Day but we are not having the other meats like we do in Dublin. It's just turkey.

"Did I tell yous that the rashers here are very salty? I could hardly eat them and they don't have the crusty turnovers or fresh loaves of bread like we do. All the bread comes already cut. They have a saying which goes, 'the best thing since sliced bread', but I think the turnovers are much nicer that you cut in big thick slices.

"In the factory, the man in charge [they call him the charge hand] goes around checking the work and things and he has to measure bits of iron and steel bars. You would never guess but when he measures what he calls steel rods like the shape of a pencil he uses a thing called a microsomething to measure how wide they are. I said to Auntie Margie that you would think that he could easily guess how big they are as they are so small. It's gas, isn't it?

"They can make great cars and clothes and have grand bands and all, and they can't guess the size of a little iron bar. Well, I have got to go. We are going to a dance in a place called the Victor Sylvester Ballroom. It's for teenagers [there's loads of teenagers in England]. I don't know what it's like but I'll let you know when I write again.

Love, Tony xxxxxx"

'You can put the turkey on the top shelf, Tom, to stop the children picking at it,' Nuala said to her husband before sitting down to a good read.

'Ok,' he answered, 'go and sit down and have a rest.'

Tom Fagan lifted the large plate on which sat the turkey carcass and stretched up to the top shelf of the airing cupboard. Sadly, he allowed the plate to tilt slightly towards himself and in so doing, caused the juices and grease to flow off the edge on to the new deep claret tie his wife had bought him for Christmas. Before he could release his frustration in a torrent of f...ing and blinding, he heard his wife calling from the other room.

'You better get the car, Tom. It's coming and I need to get to the hospital...Quick!'

Chapter 8

Da keeps telling me I'm bound to die by being burnt alive or drowning. I was really scared when the feathers on the war bonnet caught fire and then the decorations. The smell was awful. But Ma and Eileen were great and Da didn't take it too bad. Not like when me and Tony set fire to the cupboard under the stairs just to see if Da's new fire extinguisher worked. It wasn't even new, just some aul brass yoke he bought in a junk shop.

"Valuable," he said it was. "One of the first proper fire extinguishers ever to be made." God, he can be an awful eegit at times. There wasn't even any water or stuff in it, just an aul brass cylinder, empty and no good for anything. Thank God, we only put a little drop of petrol to get the fire going. But the dirty laundry that Ma put in there caught fire as well. We had an awful shaggin job putting it out. When the extinguisher didn't work, Tony and me ran getting basins and pots of water from the tap in the kitchen and throwing it on the fire.

Ma and Da were gone to the pictures, the Stella in Rathmines, to see The African Queen. *It was much feckin hotter here than in Africa, smoke everywhere and Dinny coming down from bed, and Eileen and Alana shouting and crying upstairs with the smoke and all. Sure, we were only young. I can't remember, 8 or 9 but Tony was in charge. Da gave the two of us a terrible hiding; Tony worse than me, been in charge and all, I suppose. My arse was sore for days.*

Course, we thought they wouldn't notice it when they came home. We'd left the doors and windows open to get rid of the smoke. But the mess with the burnt clothes and the water everywhere under the stairs was the worst, and the paint and wallpaper in there was all black and peeled. Couldn't blame him really for the hiding he gave us. We'd smashed the radiogram a few days before, after he'd just bought his new record. A song from the show My Fair Lady. *He loved that "On the Street where you Live" and played it for hours when he brought it home.*

But it was only the first day when he got it, then we broke the string that goes around the wheels in the back of the part where the records go. He was hopping mad.

Mind you, we were always getting hidings. Dinny went through the glass again at the bottom of the stairs. Big pane of glass; "hammered glass" they call it. But you'd imagine they'd know not to put glass like that at the bottom of the stairs. You only have to fall down the stairs or get pushed and the glass is bound to be broken.

Poor Da nearly died when he was driving up Churchtown Rd and he saw Tony and me driving the invalid carriage. Something he "picked up" he said. A black invalid carriage with three wheels, one at the front and two on the back. The engine was in the front like a motorbike and it had handlebars and gears and things. You sat in a kind of little basket hut with a hood on the top like a pram's to keep out the rain.

I don't know how Tony got it started but once he did, that was that. We stuffed Dinny in the back, right up against the hood and Tony and me got in the front seat that was like a little leather bench. It was great. We were belting it down the road and we nearly went over on all the bends until we knew how to use the brakes. We were going up and down the road for ages and then Da drove around the corner in his lorry and nearly knocked us down. What a shaggin hiding he gave us that day.

The new baby, named Rosie, eased to a large extent the ache in the hearts of her father and mother, which had been there since the deaths of their two children, Alana and the newly born baby boy. Once again, the house was filled with an infant's crying and the smell of baby sick and nappies hanging on any available peg or hook. Patsy missed only a little schooling through this particular birth as his mother came home from the hospital a few days after the school term began.

Patsy, now 14, could leave school, if he chose to, at the end of the school year, or if his parents wished it, or were unable to pay for further schooling. Patsy was troubled by his own uncertainty about what he really wanted to do. He knew his father's business was in trouble, yet he felt keenly that an exciting world was just ahead of him, but it was a world, he felt strongly, which depended on learning and knowledge. He was just discovering history and literature and he knew instinctively that to study and acquire understanding would be deeply satisfying.

But how could he be a burden on his parents' finances with a new baby and growing difficulties in selling logs and turf? He decided he would leave school in the summer and take a job. A neighbour who owned a butcher's shop in Cabra had offered him Saturday and school holiday work, and if that went well, there was a strong possibility of being an apprentice and eventually qualifying as a Master Butcher.

Patsy felt good and noble about his decision but was unprepared for his mother's reaction:

'You will not leave school. Your Da and I have already discussed the matter and you're going to carry on.'

'But Da can't afford it!'

'Never you mind that, we'll manage somehow. We're going to try for Synge St; that's a great school with the Christian Brothers, and you don't have to be rich either to go there.'

In truth, Patsy felt elated at the news. He determined he would work hard and make his parents proud of him. His friends, however, did not share his enthusiasm.

'What! Are you mad?' Reddy Costello asked.

'You must be out of your feckin skull,' added Gurky Ryan. 'You want to carry on for more schooling when you can leave and earn money and buy your own fags and all. By the time you leave, you'll be too old to do anything and we'll have jobs and know the work. We'll be way ahead of you.'

'Yeah, I know all that but even if I left this year I don't know what I want to do.'

'Just work, that's all you do,' argued Gurky. 'It doesn't matter so long as you're getting the wages. I don't give a feck what I do just so the man gives me the money on a Friday.'

'Yeah, OK, but where are you going to work?' Patsy asked.

'With me Da in the Swastika Laundry on the van,' answered Gurky.

Patsy winced at the name "Swastika", and said with bitterness, 'There's not much future in that, is there now?'

'What do you mean "future"?' Gurky replied. 'I'll be getting one pound seven and six a week without overtime, that's me future. Me and the mot going out on a Saturday night to the pictures and no shaggin school to think about.'

'And I suppose you've got it worked out as well?' Patsy said, turning to Reddy.

'I don't bleeding know yet. Maybe in the shop with me brother, or serving the petrol in Brophy's garage. Me Da said I could be a self-made man like him and be a milkman, independent and all.'

'Is that all you really want to do for all your life?' Patsy asked not managing to hide the jeering tone in his voice.

'What do you mean?' Reddy answered loudly. 'Look at you, would yeh? What are you going to do, smarty-pants? Be a spaceman and fly to the fuckin moon, or go and be a film star in all that Shakespeare shite? Jaysus, you're getting very big for your boots. You haven't got into Synge Street yet you know.'

Patsy was sorry over the argument with his friends and decided to avoid telling them again about his plans for his future.

I didn't mean to hurt Reddy's feelings. What future? Sure, I don't know about me own future. I'm an awful ballocks annoying them like that. Let them do what they want and don't be jeering them. Well, I didn't mean to; it just came out like that. Shite, you just think you're better. What a terrible name for a laundry, "Swastika"; you'd think the government would ban a name like that. Still, we were neutral so I suppose it's not right for us to ban it.

That's feckin shite and you know it. If the man who owns that laundry was decent, he'd change it. Or people could tell him to change the name or they wouldn't use his laundry. Mr Bambrick said it'd been the Swastika Laundry since the beginning of the century before anyone heard of Hitler or Nazis. But we know about them now and what they did so we shouldn't have their feckin badge on a Dublin laundry.

Chapter 9

He was spending the weekend with his cousin Billy O'Hara. His Auntie Maisie had asked his mother if she would let him come out to Finglas and Nuala Fagan had agreed, knowing how much Patsy liked his older cousin, and she was keen to find little treats for Patsy because of the way he had again managed the household when she had gone into hospital to have Rosie.

Billy O'Hara was 16 but looked older. His face could remind you of a dry, dirty-greyish-white dishcloth that only came to life when it was full of liquid, usually beer in the case of Billy. He met Patsy at the bus stop in Finglas and the two walked together to Cappa Rd where Billy lived.

'Well, me auld, Patsy, how are you?'

'Ah, grand thanks, and how's yourself?'

'Right as rain, especially when I can get a few bevies inside meself.'

'You're not still drinking all that porter, are you? What does your Ma say?'

'She doesn't say anything. Just gives me a good fuckin box in the face when she sees me plastered.'

'And what about your da?'

'He roars and shouts but sure he's always out working. And when he's home, he's sleeping and I'm gone to work. I just make sure I don't see him when he gets home at night.'

'And do you not get thrown out of the pubs cause you're not old enough?'

'No, I don't. I look older. Me Da says I could pass for 40 if I wanted to. Anyway, you'll have to look older when we go into town tonight. We'll go to Mooney's on the Quays to have a gargle before we go to the pictures. Did you ask that feckin eegit Gurky to meet us?'

'Yeah, he's going to be at the Pillar at 7'clock.'

'Ah great, he's a good shaggin laugh, that Gurky.'

They played football on the grassy green in front of Billy's house and wrestled with Billy's friends and neighbours in a ball game that was a mixture of football and rugby. Some of the girls in the area often joined in these games, and Patsy, along with the other boys, always welcomed the opportunity of wrestling with the girls.

'Jesus up in Heaven above, did you see the diddies on that Maureen Kelly?' Billy asked when they were having their tea.

'Yeah,' said Patsy. 'I didn't only see them, I got a good feel of them. She nearly bit the shaggin hand off me. Said I was hurting her and she told me to feck off for meself. But she's really gorgeous.'

'Don't fall in love with every mot you see, Patsy. There's millions of them out there and they're all waiting for a good fella to look after them.'

They met Gurky Ryan at Nelson's Pillar and headed up O'Connell St towards the Liffey and then turned left for Mooney's pub.

'Now yous two listen,' said Billy. 'Try to shaggin look older and if the barman says anything, just say you're 18. I'll ask for the drinks at the bar and yous can give me the money later.'

The three boys took stools at the bar where a barman looked at them with more than a little doubt.

'Well, gentlemen,' he said, 'will it be lemonade or milk? Which?'

'Three glasses of porter,' said Billy O'Hara.

'Maybe one glass for yourself,' answered the barman. 'But not for the two children here. Are they your two sons?'

'No, they're feckin not. They're 18 the twos of them. C'mon give us three glasses.'

'I will not. They can have lemonade, and get away from the bar in that corner over there before I throw the three of you out and call the Guarda.'

They sat in the dark corner sipping their drinks with Billy who was feeling annoyed.

'Feckin ballocks of a culchie. Think they own the place. Up from the arsehole of the country and they want to take over our city. Anyway, I told yous to try and look older. Look at that shaggin gansey you're wearing Gurky. Nobody except a kid would wear something like that.'

'What's wrong with it? Anyway, it's the only one I've got,' said an obviously offended Gurky.

'It doesn't matter about the beer,' said Patsy.

'Course it does,' argued Billy. 'Anyway, we'll go to Kavanagh's after the pictures and we'll get a drink there. But this time, you and Gurky go to a table and sit down with your backs to the bar and I'll get the drinks, OK?'

'Ok,' Gurky replied, 'but I only want a lemonade.'

'You'll have a proper shaggin drink, you will,' ordered Billy. 'Where did you get that name "Gurky"? Never heard it on anybody else.'

'Me real name's George,' answered Gurky, 'and when I was little, everybody called me "Georgie", but me baby brother couldn't say that, so he called me "Gurky" and everyone called me Gurky since.'

The film was *Jailhouse Rock* and they moved and swayed to the music and singing as though hypnotised and in a trance.

'Isn't Elvis great?' Gurky said.

'Shaggin brilliant,' Billy answered.

'Yeah, it was good,' said Patsy, 'but I preferred him in *Love Me Tender*.'

'There you go again,' Billy teased. 'I bet it was the mot you fell in love with, didn't you?'

The visit to Kavanagh's pub proved successful in that Patsy and Gurky got their Guinness porter. Patsy said he could not drink more Guinness after two glasses. Billy convinced him that the best thing to take away the taste of the Guinness and make him feel better was to drink some cider.

'Are you sure it's OK?' Patsy asked.

'Of course me aul bowsie. It's just like Cidona. You've had that before, haven't you?'

'Oh yeah, that's OK. I like that Cidona.'

'And me,' Gurky called out. 'I'll have some of that Cidona as well.'

'Sure yous are great drinkers,' concluded Billy O'Hara.

They left Gurky at the bottom of Grafton St and watched him set off towards Stephen's Green dancing between the oncoming cars playing his imaginary guitar. He was wriggling his hips in sharp jerky movements and their last sight of him was in the middle of the street as he passed the Brown Thomas store, knees splayed Elvis style, arching upwards onto the points of his shoes and his right hand strumming wildly his guitar as passing motorists told him in very clear language what to do with his guitar and Elvis Presley.

Patsy and Billy took the bus back to Finglas. Patsy was feeling warm and wonderful and witty, and he winked and smiled when he caught some young girl's eye on the bus. By the time they reached Finglas Village, his enhanced happiness had taken a rather bad turn and he was feeling very sick. Billy held him by the backs of his legs as he leant over a parapet wall to vomit and try to die.

'I see you've taken to drinking, Patsy Fagan.'

The loud penetrating voice of his uncle Bill woke him harshly the next morning.

'Ah well,' continued his uncle, 'it's a great thing that a man can go out and enjoy himself and take a few glasses without being a nuisance to others. Are you one of those, Patsy?'

'I don't know, Uncle Bill,' groaned a far from well Patsy.

'You aren't one of those who gets soft in the head and starts shouting and fighting and ends up getting sick, are you?'

'I hope not, Uncle Bill.'

'Take my advice, Patsy, and leave the gargle alone for a few years, or you'll end up like the poor auld gobshite in the bed there beside you.'

'What's that, Da?' enquired a not entirely sober Billy O'Hara from beneath the blankets.

'Get up the pair of yous and come down for your breakfast. And then go off to Mass and ask God for forgiveness.'

He left his cousin in the afternoon and took the bus back to the city, getting off at Parnell Sq so he could enjoy a walk through the centre of Dublin. The icy February air discouraged most would-be strollers, but Patsy pulled his navy blue gabardine coat tighter around himself and braved the wet freezing wind that blew from the east carrying with it its usual salty taste of the Irish Sea. He stood and looked up at the monument of Charles Stewart Parnell and read the familiar words of the inscription:

"No man has a right to fix the boundary to the march of a nation. No man has a right to say to his country: Thus far thou go and no further…"

Hello Parnell, or Chief, if you prefer. That's what they called you when you were alive. It's a grand monument they built you but it's a pity that not everybody here in Ireland wants you to have one. Me Da says the church broke your heart and your spirit. Mr Bambrick says you got mixed up with another man's wife and the newspapers in England crucified you until you got very sick and died.

Da says you were a fool to try and win freedom for a Catholic country that preached that Protestants could not even get into heaven just because they are

Protestants. It's strange that we have two Protestant cathedrals and only a pro-cathedral for the Catholics. "Pro" is Latin meaning "for" when you want to say "instead of" or "standing in for", I think.

She must've been very beautiful. Old Bambo said her name was Kitty O'Shea. Must've been Irish with a name like that. Was she a Protestant too? And Parnell was born in County Wicklow. Would me Da call him a culchie? He was Anglo-Irish aristocracy, that's what Bambo said. But does that mean he's an Anglo-Irish culchie? How can you have a Protestant culchie? Maybe you can, otherwise all those Protestants who are living in country areas today are not culchies. Then what are they? What are culchies?

Me Da says they are muck savages living in the arsehole of the country, and Billy O'Hara calls them rednecks and wildmen who wear trousers that are about a yard wide at the bottom. But that's silly. I've been to the country lots of times and I've never seen savages like Da says or wild men that Billy talks about. Ma says it's just that Dubliners are jealous of the country people because they are better educated than themselves, and Dubliners don't find it as easy to cheat country people as they do to cheat each other. An awful lot of our heroes came from the country or even from other countries.

Sister Agnes told us it was a sin to go into a Protestant church. For years when I was little, I always turned me head away when I passed St Patrick's Cathedral or Christ Church. Me Da said she was a bad minded old cow and Ma said she couldn't understand how Sister Agnes could say things like that when so many of Ireland's great writers, as well as its heroes and leaders against the English, were Protestant. She used to put a big, white sheet of paper on the blackboard with drawing pins.

"This is your soul, children, when you are spotless, like Our Lady, except of course, you can't be like Our Lady because she was immaculate. But your soul, which God gives you, as part of himself, is like this lovely, clean sheet of gleaming white paper. But if you commit a venial sin, this is what happens to your soul."

And she put a brown mark on the gleaming white paper with a brown crayon.

"And if you commit lots of venial sins, this is what happens." And she put marks and smudges and all everywhere on the white paper so it looked dirty.

"What's a venial sin, Sister Agnes?"

"You should know the answer to that! It's when you don't say your prayers at night or don't do what your parents tell you, or don't give a proper bow of your head when you pass a priest in the street."

"How many kinds of sin is there, Sister Agnes?"

"I don't know what I'm teaching you if you don't know the answer to that question."

"I forgot, Sister."

"If I gave you a good belt of the stick you wouldn't forget, would you?"

"No, Sister."

"Well, you remember this time. There are two main kinds of sins, 'venial' and 'mortal'. Now I've given examples of venial sins, but who can tell me what a mortal sin is?"

"It's when you do something that **really** offends Our Lord or His Holy Church, and if you die with a mortal sin on your soul, you'll go straight to Hell."

"Good. I'm glad to see someone is learning their lessons. Who can give me examples of a mortal sin?"

"Cursing a priest, Sister."

"Murdering someone."

"Stealing from a blind man."

"Not putting enough money on the plate at Mass."

"Looking at your sister when she's putting on her frock."

"Not blessing yourself when you go past a church."

"Listening to your Da when he's saying curses about the priest or Our Holy Father, Pope Pius XII."

"All of those are very good examples of mortal sins, and this is what your soul looks like if you commit one."

And she took a heavy black crayon and rubbed black all over the whole, white, gleaming sheet, until it was just full of black and no white left anywhere.

When I was older, I asked Sister Carmel about it and she told me I must try to understand Sister Agnes's "little ways", and she didn't mean any harm. And, of course, Robert Emmet and other good Protestants could go to Heaven if they deserved to, just like Catholics, but you'd get there quicker if you were a Catholic. She said it was alright for me to go into St Patrick's and Christ Church but I shouldn't tell Sister Agnes about it.

Funny if you think about what Sister Agnes believes: You have Robert Emmet and Wolf Tone and Jonathan Swift in Hell, and Patrick Pearse and Michael Collins and Kevin Barry in Heaven.

You'll be with the first lot, Charles Stewart Parnell, so what do you think of that me "uncrowned King of Ireland"?

Chapter 10

Patsy's father bought his son a bicycle as a reward for looking after the family when Nuala had gone into hospital to have her eight child. It was a second-hand bicycle.

'Almost new, a Raleigh racer,' Tom Fagan said.

'It's not a racer,' said Dinny, 'cause it hasn't got the drop-down handlebars.'

'It's a semi-racer with straight handlebars,' said his father, 'with three speed gears.'

'Yeah, but it's not a real racer,' insisted Dinny.

'You don't know what you're talking about, you little get,' argued Tom.

'Raleigh is the Rolls Royce of bikes and this model is the Rolls Royce of semi-racers. So there Smart-Alec what do you make of that?'

'It's not a racer,' Dinny said.

Patsy loved the bike and did not care whether it was a full racing bicycle or not. It was sky-blue and sleek, and as far as he was concerned, the best bike in Landscape Avenue. He could not wait to try it out and was soon riding up and down the roads in Churchtown, head and shoulders bent over the handlebars, peddling furiously, and in his mind, winning every race under the sun.

Others were waiting for their ride on the new second-hand bike but Patsy would only allow them a lift on the crossbar. First in line was Dinny; Patsy took him down past the little glen with the stream running through it, on to the smooth tarmac road which led down the steep hill to the River Dodder. Dinny was in glory shouting out to friends in the streets and yelping whenever he took a sharp bump on the bottom as he bounced on the steel crossbar.

'Jeeze, it's great, Patsy. I wish I had a semi-racer as well. It's much better than Reddy's aul bike.'

'You'll have one when you're older and then we can have races.'

His sister, Eileen, wanted her go on the crossbar but preferred to sit on the saddle, legs spreadeagle, while Patsy stood up on the pedals and cycled in an upright position. Reddy Costello was predictably jealous but tried not to show it.

'I prefer drop-handlebars and six gears. Me Ma says maybe next Christmas I can have one.'

'Ah, that's great,' Patsy answered, 'but next Christmas is a long way off, nearly nine months.'

Reddy's envy grew considerably when he saw Patsy cycling along Churchtown Road with Catherine Sullivan sat on the crossbar, her hands holding Patsy's wrists as he steered the bike, her long auburn hair blowing into Patsy's face, and her creamy freckled face turning to look up at Patsy with what appeared to be total adoration.

Much as Patsy loved her looking at him with her bright green eyes and her wide smile, showing perfect white teeth, he preferred, at least when she was on the crossbar, that she should look ahead in front of her so that he could lean forward and rest his chin on her shoulder, and the side of his face would touch her neck and his nose could nestle in her hair. He could smell the soap on her skin and the smoky-wood perfume of her hair.

Her breath was visible in the cold air of the early spring morning and Patsy saw her as a shining, bright angel, born to bring happiness to him. In his imagination, she was his Juliet, his Sarah Curran, his Kitty O'Shea. Patsy felt himself to be in love with this convent-educated Catherine who was always perfect in every way: her dresses were always immaculately clean; her white ankle socks were tight and never sagged, and when she wore her fawn knee-length socks as part of her school uniform, they sat straight and snug without crease or fold.

He could find no fault with her, and as he cycled towards Rathfarham, with her on his crossbar, laughing and talking and telling each other jokes, he believed himself to be the luckiest fellow in the whole of Ireland.

She had agreed to go to the cinema with him the previous week and he had felt elated and triumphant because all the 14 and 15-year-old boys in the neighbourhood had been chasing after Catherine Sullivan who was also 14. She had refused all offers and approaches until now, but when Patsy came to her house to swap comics with her and her two younger sisters, he whispered the invitation into her ear to go with him to the pictures. She would have to ask her mother but if given permission she would love to go with him.

Her mother consented but they were to come straight home after the film and were not to "malinger" around and get up to no good. Patsy told none of his friends of his victory, for he knew that to do so would be to invite their comments about every aspect of his new-found treasure. He dreaded particularly what Reddy might say about her "diddies", or rather the very visible lack of them.

That's all the feckin eegit can think about. He wouldn't admit he was jealous or he'd been trying for months to go out with her. Anyway, they'll soon grow on her and she'll be even more gorgeous.

They walked to the Dundrum picture house in the cold, darkening evening. She was wearing a red waisted coat that went down to her knees and had black buttons and a short black belt at the back, which was purely for decoration. She wore a black woollen hat pulled tightly over on her head and her long hair served as a scarf around her shoulders and neck.

As Patsy shyly took her hand when they were out of sight of their parents' houses, he felt the warmth of her gloved hand within his own and thrilled as she returned the pressure of his grip.

If ever a film had been made to suit Patsy's mood and his view of the world, it was Wuthering Heights. They sat, hand in hand, entranced; they themselves lived in the film from minute to minute and second to second; they felt Heathcliff's anger with Hindley and shared in his love of Cathy; they refused to believe Cathy could love Earnshaw no matter how good a man he was, and they cried a little, despite their efforts not to, when Heathcliff came to his Cathy on her deathbed and held her in his arms, speaking the terrible and wonderful words to her of his love and passion as she was dying.

The two young would be lovers sat mesmerised, hanging on to every half syllable and utterance of the two lovers on the screen:

"What do they know of heaven or hell, Cathy, who know nothing of life? Oh, they're praying for you, Cathy. I'll pray one prayer with them I'll repeat till my tongue stiffens: Catherine Earnshaw, may you not rest while I live on. I killed you. Haunt me, then! Haunt your murderer! I know that ghosts have wandered on the earth. Be with me always—take any form—drive me mad! Only do not leave me in this dark alone where I cannot find you. I cannot live without my life! I cannot die without my soul…"

Patsy told her that he would be going up to the turf cuttings in the Easter holidays with his father, and Eileen and Dinny would also come along, and probably Gurky Ryan as well. They could make a picnic and stay there all day and it would be great fun and could she please, please come with them. On a bright, warm Saturday morning, Eileen Fagan and Catherine Sullivan took their places in the cab next to Eileen's father, Tom, who would drive them to the very top of the Dublin Mountains. Patsy, Dinny and Gurky Ryan were in the back of the former Jacob's biscuit van, now an open pick-up truck, following Tom Fagan's "conversion" of it.

'So that it's not so high on the back that you can't get down the driveways with the branches and all,' Tom Fagan had explained. The boys were sat on hessian sacks with their backs tight against the wooden slats, which Tom Fagan had fitted when he converted the van into a pickup. Patsy had hoped that Catherine Sullivan would have sat in the back with him but his father had been firm.

'She can sit up front with your sister, Eileen, so that the poor creature doesn't have to put up with the three of yous gawping at her, and that dope Gurky Ryan asking her silly questions which he doesn't even understand the meaning of.'

They drove up through Rathfarnham to the foothills of the mountains:

'That's where Ma and Da got married,' shouted Patsy as they passed the Church of the Annunciation.

'I just knew you were going to say that,' said Dinny, 'cause every time we pass it you roar out like a madman, "That's where me Ma and Da got married". Honest to Jesus, you'd get on anybody's nerves.'

'You're a gas man, Dinny,' said Gurky Ryan, 'telling off your older brother. And I bet you tell off your sister, Eileen, as well, do you?'

'She knows you're after her, Gurky Ryan,' answered Dinny, 'but she thinks you're a right amadan. She says all Patsy's pals are eegits who have nothing better to do than listen to Elvis Presley and stare at any mot who walks past and saying dirty things about them.'

'We're not like that, are we, Patsy?' Gurky asked.

'No, we're not. As Uncle Bill says, we're "gentlemen and scholars".'

They continued on the narrow steep roads that took them through Ballyboden and Woodtown towards the summit of Mountpelier. The boys look silently at the ruin of the 18c hunting-lodge which had become so infamous as the mountain headquarters of the Hell Fire Club. Patsy could not help but allow a comparison with Hindley's house in *Wuthering Heights* to enter his mind. They passed through the dark green of the Pine Forest and took the tiny road that led into the boggy turf cuttings.

Tom Fagan parked his truck on one of the white gravel tracks that had been laid and reinforced at the end of the 19th century to cater for the weight of the horse-drawn carts which had come out from Dublin to transport the turf back to the city. As always, the first thing to do was to run and jump on the springy, peaty surface of the bogland.

'It's better than any aul mattress,' screamed Dinny, giving a good imitation of a gymnast on a trampoline.

'Da, can we go for a walk and explore before we cut the turf?' Patsy asked.

'There'll be plenty of time for that later on, but first, we'll cut and stand the turf in small wigwam piles for drying. Eileen and Catherine can arrange the food and stuff and when we've had some dinner, we'll load the truck with the dry turf from the big stack to take back down to the yard. Then yous can wander and play all yous want but be careful not to fall into any pools. They're deep mind you and you could drown easily enough. Did you hear me, Dinny?'

Patsy's father had his own turf banks that he rented from Wicklow County Council at £5 per bank per annum. He had no map to show him where his banks were but each of the unclassified gravel roads had a marker at its head which had a number on it and each turf bank along a particular road also had a number to identify it. Tom Fagan had been issued with two turf bank dockets each valued at £5 and each with two numbers indicating gravel road and turf bank. Trenches were cut into the turf bank which could be as wide as five feet and as deep as ten.

Eventually, the trenches would join together leaving an area of bog that had been stripped of several feet or yards of good turf depending on the depth. The cutter would stand in the narrow trenches and use a long-handled spade called a slane to slice through the soaking blocks of turf, and in the same movement would swing the slane upwards and land the sodden turf onto the edge of the trench above.

Those working on top would lift the wet blocks and place them on a flatbed wheelbarrow and take them to the end of the bank and stand them in wigwam-shaped piles to allow the wind to pass through them so they would dry quickly. The cutters and carriers had to be careful not to allow the delicate wet blocks to break into pieces. As the turf blocks dried in the wind, they became very hard and could stand up to a good many knocks and rough handling without breaking.

Tom Fagan took great pride in his skill at cutting the blocks and heaving them to the surface on the end of his slane without breaking them. His sons equally were proud of their father's ability and also took pride in their own in being able to cart and stack the blocks without damaging them. Soon the father and sons and Gurky Ryan found a co-ordinated rhythm of working together and there was a continuous posse of boys carting blocks to form small wigwams of turf along the white gravel track.

Eileen and Catherine had gone to gather pieces of bone-dry turf to burn on their picnic fire. They also collected some wild bog plants and yellow bladderwort flowers. They picked butterworts, sundews and cotton grass to embroider their picnic space. They made a round fire bed of flint stones found along the gravel road and using newspaper from Tom Fagan's truck and dried bramble and gorse, they soon had the pieces of turf glowing red and burning slowly, giving off a gentle, woody smelling smoke.

When the time came, they took the cardboard box with food, plates, cutlery and large cast-iron frying pan out of the truck, and spread a white bedsheet, serving as a tablecloth, which Eileen's mother, Nuala, had packed. The frying pan was nestled on the flint stones and Eileen spooned in a large lump of beef dripping that sizzled and melted immediately. Sausages followed and then pieces of smoked bacon, and these were placed in an enamel roasting dish at the edge of the fire.

Cut slices of black and white pudding spat and splashed in the hot pan and chopped onions and wild mushrooms were added. Catherine filled a blackened kettle with water from one of the countless, tiny, freshwater streams bordering the turf banks and placed it on the fire to boil. She cut thick slices of crusty loaf and spread the butter generously. When the kettle boiled, she spooned in the loose tealeaves that Nuala had put in a brown paper bag.

When all was ready, the two young girls waved at the turf bank some forty yards away, shouting for boys and man to come to dinner. One call was all that was needed, and the little group sat on the dry warm turf with sausage, bacon, black and white pudding sandwiches, bulging with mushrooms and fried onions, dripping fat and melting butter onto their plates. Catherine served them tin mugs of hot, sweet tea to wash down the food.

'Who cooked these sausages?' Gurky Ryan asked, fully aware of the answer. 'Jaysus, they're lovely, best I've ever eaten.'

'I did,' said a blushing Eileen.

'And this tea is great,' said Patsy. 'Who made it?'

'Me,' said a smiling Catherine.

'Just seems like any aul tea and sausages and all to me,' said Dinny. 'I don't know what yous two are making all the fuss about.'

When they finished their meal, they loaded dried turf into the back of the truck but leaving sufficient room for the three boys to lie or sit on the load on the way back to the city without falling off onto the road.

'Now yous can go and have a wander or play if yous want. I'm going to sit down and read the paper and maybe have a little nap,' said Tom Fagan.

The five walked in the same direction along a white gravel track until they reached another track turning off to the left.

'Let's split up,' said Patsy, 'and meet back in an hour at Da's lorry.'

'Who's going with who?' Eileen asked.

There was a silence as each one waited for someone else to suggest the groupings.

'Catherine and I'll go together,' said Eileen. 'And yous three can make a nuisance of yourselves on your own.'

'No, that's not right,' answered Patsy, a little more urgently than he had intended. 'There should be a boy in each group to protect the girl.'

'Oh my Jesus,' said Dinny, 'I wish I'd stayed with Da.'

'Ok,' said Eileen laughing. 'I'll protect Dinny and Gurky, and you, Patsy Fagan, can protect the fair Catherine. Does that suit you now?'

'That's fine,' said Patsy with a business-like tone. 'Let's go then, Catherine.'

She stood there, blushing slightly, and looking mischievously at Dinny.

'Are you sure you don't want to come with us, Dinny?' she called.

'Naw,' he answered back. 'I don't want to get in the way.'

'But you don't shaggin mind getting in my way, you little get,' Gurky Ryan whispered into his ear as he held him in a headlock.

Patsy took Catherine's hand, but she pulled it away.

'Your dad might see us,' she protested.

'Not up here, he won't. Look, Catherine, see those rocks. I'll race you!'

And he was off ahead of her and she followed in his footsteps, running wildly across the marshy surface, leaping over small bog pools and skirting around the wild ferns. They reached the rocky outcrop, laughing and breathing hard, their breath showing in the cooling mountain air.

'This could be our Wuthering Heights, Catherine,' said an excited Patsy.

'And you, Patsy, and are you going to run away and make your fortune and come back and find me?'

'Do you want me to go away?'

'Of course not, but the true hero must do brave deeds and have great adventures if the girl is going to love him madly.'

'What brave things can I do, Catherine?'

'Can you climb to the very top of these rocks and shout as loud as you can, "Catherine Sullivan, the finest of all her sex and the pride of nature!".'

'Of course, I can; watch!'

And he scrambled up the rocks and stood on the highest boulder and shouted her words in every direction.

'What else can I do?' he called.

'Come down, Patsy, before you kill yourself.'

'I would die happily for you, Catherine,' he told her when he reached her side.

'Would you, Patsy, would you die for me? Would you love me like Heathcliff loved Cathy, so that nothing could ever hurt me?'

'I would Catherine, I would, you know I would.'

'Well, close your eyes and count up to ten.'

He closed his eyes and before he reached ten, chaste and innocent lips met in the lightest of kisses. He remained completely still, eyes closed waiting for her to kiss him again, and when she did not, he opened his eyes, and she was gone. He looked around and saw her in the distance, running in the direction they had come.

'Wait for me,' he shouted. 'I love you.'

She stopped and turned around.

'Prove it. If you catch me before we get back, I'll believe you!'

He ran as fast as he could, jumping over turf trenches and across narrow bog pools. He fell and scrambled and grazed his hands and knees. He knew he was gaining ground on her but she was a fine athlete, and she was also determined he would not catch her. He was desperate to go faster; there were only a few hundred yards to go and he could see his father's truck clearly now.

He saw the turf cutting ahead of him and the bog pool alongside of it. He knew it was an easy jump for him to clear it, only four or five feet in width. He took it in full flight and his right foot landed firmly on the far bank of the pool, but the soft ground beneath his left foot collapsed and Patsy found himself toppling backwards and then sliding down into the hole. He landed chest deep in the cloying boggy pool.

The peaty growth below his feet was soft and yielding and he dared not move for fear of sinking deeper. Catherine's face appeared above him, looking anxious.

'Hang on, Patsy, I'll get your dad.'

Five minutes later, Tom Fagan, Dinny, Eileen, Gurky and Catherine were all stood around the hole, looking down at him. His father lay down at the edge of the pool and lowered his long-handled slane. Patsy took hold of the right-angled blade and his father pulled gently. He came up little by little with a squelchy "plop" at first, until his father took hold of his wrist, and he knew he was safe.

'Where are your shoes, Patsy?' Gurky asked.

When Patsy looked at their faces, they were all laughing heartily and enjoying the hilarity of his misfortune. And his own Catherine joined in the fun. She had lost a little of her perfection in our hero's eyes.

Chapter 11

"I'm telling you, you'll drown or burn to death one of these days." When did Da *first say that? After the bicycle tyre, or after the fire under the stairs, or when Tony and me put the piece of burning newspaper in the petrol tank of the invalid carriage? I don't know. When I was very young, I think. And I don't know when I started drowning meself neither.*

Not up in the bog that's for sure. It was a long time before that. They were all laughing up in the bog, all of them, including her. It was funny though, no matter what.

*"I wasn't laughing **at** you,"* she told me that and she was angry with me for *been so serious and moody and all.*

"We were all just relieved and happy that you were safe. I thought you were going to drown, Patsy."

Drowning again. I know the first time, or the first serious time at least. I was about 7 and it was down in the canal. It took Da four months to find the soldier. He went all over Harold's Cross talking to everybody.

"Did you see the soldier?"

"Of course I did, Tom; he was a young fella with black curly hair."

"But how do you know he was a soldier?"

"Cause he was wearing a soldier's uniform. For Christ's sake, Tom Fagan, how else would I feckin know?"

"Did the soldier say anything to you?"

"No. What would he say? Wasn't he exhausted and soaking wet?"

"Did you see what rank he was?"

"Rank me arse. He was only in his trousers and vest. His rank isn't tattooed on his arm you know."

"You don't need to find him, Tom Fagan. It's good enough for you to know what he's done."

*"I **do** need to find him. I want to thank him and give him something."*

"He'll get his thanks in heaven. You should say the rosary every week for him that he doesn't have to stay in Purgatory too long."

"Do you know what barracks he belonged to?"

"No."

"Tell me what he looked like again."

"He was a young fella in his twenties or early thirties, a bit skinny with black curly hair."

"I'm telling you once and for all, Tom Fagan, and I would appreciate it if you would wash out your ears and listen, because I am not going to tell you again, you Jackeen. I made enquiries and discovered that the soldier was walking over Harold's Cross Bridge, and he saw the commotion. He took off his tunic, hat and boots and laid them on the bank and dived in. When it was all over, he was gone, disappeared, vanished into thin air."

Da repeated all these things to me for years afterwards. He was very fond of telling me what his friend, Detective Sergeant Dan O'Connell, from Rathgar Guarda Station, told him about washing out his ears and all and what Da said to him.

"I told him I'd find the soldier meself and I didn't need the help of a big Cork culchie redneck who couldn't detect shite in a lavatory pot." We were always jumping onto the edge of the canal barges when they came under the bridge at Harold's Cross. The canal was narrow there and you could leap on to the wooden buffer-rail that ran along the side of the boat at about the same level as the canal banks.

You hung on to the edge of the deck with your hands, with your foot on the rail, and before the boat got out into the wide bit of the canal away from the bank, you shoved yourself back with a good push off the boat to get back on to the bank. You had to stay on the boat as long as you could and make the biggest jump. Gurky, Reddy and me were all hanging on the boat at the same time, and the man kept shouting and cursing at us to get the fuck off, and what he was going to do to us when he caught us and all.

Reddy was always getting the boatmen annoyed, calling them fat lazy ballockses, and they'd rush over to get us and we'd jump back to the bank before they caught us. They were always saying they'd jump off and run after us and give us a good box in the ears when they caught us. But they never jumped off.

On that day, I stayed on too long and I missed the bank, just like up in the bog. It was a very peaceful sort of floating feeling. I didn't feel the water going into me or anything, and I wasn't cold like you would be if you'd just dived in. I didn't know anything, just dreamy floating. They said me wellington boots dragged me down out of the way of the barge and its propeller, and that probably stopped me getting a serious injury. I knew something was happening to me when I felt meself being dragged and pushed, like when we're in a fight in school.

It was the soldier dragging me from the bottom of the canal to the surface and then on to the canal bank. Then he was sitting on me and pressing down on me chest to get the water out of me. I was coughing like mad and all, and then I was crying. There was a woman who said I looked just like death. I could see Gurky and Reddy on the other bank of the canal and they were crying as well.

Someone shouted, "His mam's here." And I saw me Ma bending down over me.

"Is he yours, Missis?"

"Jesus, Mary and Joseph help me," I heard Ma say. "He is mine, God help me. What've you being doing, Patsy? Could somebody help me to get him up onto the bridge please. I've got the baby in the pram up there and I'll put this fella on the top and take him home. Jesus, what's your Da going to say? He'll murder you, he will."

I was lifted and carried up to the pram that Ma had left on the footpath on the bridge. Alana was only a little baby and they put me on the end of the pram and Ma wheeled us home. I was in bed when Da came in and I heard them talking in the kitchen. Ma was telling Da that they told her I'd been in the water for about three or four minutes and a soldier dived in but he couldn't find me as the water was so dirty.

He had to keep diving in until he could feel me and they all expected me to be dead and all because I was in there for so long. Da came in and sat on the side of the bed.

"Are you awake, Patsy?"

I was pretending to be asleep and I didn't say nothing. Da lay down beside me and put his arms around me and I fell asleep.

He found the soldier at last. One of the officers in Portobello Barracks heard that a soldier had saved a boy in the canal and the Da was looking for him to say thanks and all. Someone told the officer that a lieutenant had come in one day soaking wet and it hadn't even been raining or anything. The officer asked the lieutenant if it was him who saved me and he admitted it was but he didn't want any reward. Da tried to give him money but he wouldn't take it.

In the end, Da bought him a thousand cigarettes and the soldier took them and thanked Da, but said there was no need, and it had been a pleasure to save me.

They heard all about me nearly drowning in school and they made an awful fuss over me. Sister Carmel gave me some Clarnico-Murray chocolates and the Reverend Mother brought me in liquorice sticks and said it was a miracle I was alive, and God must've chosen me for a special favour. Gurky Ryan asked her what the favour was that God wanted from me. Sister Agnes looked at me and told me I'd been a lot of trouble to many people. She hoped that me Da had dealt with me properly and taught me a good lesson.

"He said I'm going to Tara St swimming baths to learn to swim like a fish, Sister."

I didn't mean to annoy her but she just gave me a box in the ears. All in all though, it was grand people making the fuss over me and giving me chocolates and all and telling me how lucky I was. I thought they meant lucky about getting the sweets and things.

Poor Reddy and Gurky got a good hiding from their das for nearly causing me death.

"It was your own fault for staying on the boat too long," said Reddy. "You nearly drown and then you get loads of sweets and chocolates and everybody feeling sorry for you and what do I get? I didn't fall in and lose me wellington boots or cause the soldier all the trouble and nearly give me Ma a heart attack, and I get a good feckin hiding from me da."

At school, Mr Bambrick's voice did not allow for too much daydreaming.

'Right, who's got the first question? You, Costello, let's have it.'

'Me Da says there can't be a god if He lets bad things happen.'

'What bad things did he have in mind?' the schoolteacher asked.

'He said he couldn't understand how any decent God could let the airplane crash with the Manchester United football team on it.'

'Would anyone like to give Master Costello a view on this?'

'What about all the other accidents that Jesus lets happen?' Gurky Ryan shouted.

'And people being killed and starving to death?'

'Father McKenna says Jesus loves us all and even the hairs on our head is more important than all the sparrows put together,' said Noel Browne.

'I think him and his Ma kisses Father McKenna's arse every day,' Reddy whispered to Patsy.

'Then why did Jesus let Tommy Taylor and Bill Whelan die in that plane crash?' Gurky Ryan shouted at Noel Browne.

'And Bobby Charlton,' called another voice.

'He didn't die, you amadan,' half a dozen boys answered together.

'He got hurt, didn't he?' Gurky said taking up the argument. 'It's the same thing. He got lots of pain and suffering and Jesus is responsible.'

'Don't be stupid,' answered Noel Browne. 'Jesus isn't responsible.'

'He could've stopped it happening, couldn't He, if He wanted to?' Gurky replied.

'Why didn't He, Sir?' a boy asked.

'Cause He can't,' called out another.

'Maybe Jesus doesn't care,' another boy shouted.

'Ok, boys,' said Mr Bambrick, 'let's take the main issue that Reddy Costello raised. I think the best way we can understand that issue is to put the question something like this: 'When terrible things happen to people, such as the airplane crash in Munich, in February, when Manchester United footballers were killed and terribly injured, why does Our Lord, because He's all powerful and merciful, not stop these awful things happening?'

'That's exactly right, Sir,' said Reddy.

'Thank you, Costello. Now listen, boys, I want you all to imagine a world in which there is absolutely no danger.'

'Ah, Jaysus, that'd be great,' called out Gurky Ryan. 'Does that mean, Sir, that you'd never even get a hiding from your da?'

'Don't take the name of Our Lord in vain, Master Ryan, or you'll be getting a hiding from me.'

'There you are, Gurky, there's danger in this classroom and Our Lord won't save you from it. Will He, Sir?' Reddy Costello shouted.

'That'll do, thank you, Costello. Now if we lived in a world where God interfered and stopped everybody from being hurt or killed all the time, then there would be no risks at all, and I don't think that's the sort of world we would want to live in.'

'What would be wrong with a world like that?' Patsy asked.

'I'm coming to that, Master Fagan. Think about what human beings are like. How they live together. What ambitions they have. A hundred years ago, it took as long as six months to get to Australia in a sailing ship. The conditions were terrible and many people got sick and died.

'People took risks crossing oceans because they *wanted* to go to Australia and build better lives for themselves. That was their ambition—to achieve something good but there were great risks. Nowadays, we manufacture an aluminium tube and we put wings and great powerful jet engines on it which hurl the tube through the skies at three, four and even five hundred miles an hour, full of men, women and children.

'So now you can get to Australia in two or three days and that's better than six months on the open sea, but it's still risky. Flying in airplanes at such high speeds means almost certain death if it crashes, and some people refuse to do it because they are afraid of the risk and they don't go. They stay behind. Now when something is safe to do with no risk or danger, then you don't feel any sense of real achievement in it.

'You don't feel pride that you've done something difficult, that you've overcome obstacles and hardships. When Hillary reached the top of Mount Everest, think how he must have felt. How do you think he felt?'

'He must've felt smashing cause he was the first man to get to the top,' answered Patsy.

'I bet he felt great,' shouted Gurky.

'I bet he said a prayer of thanks to God,' said Noel Browne.

'Prayer me arse. I bet he felt feckin shagged out after all that climbing,' Reddy Costello called out.

'Costello! Stand at the back of the class, you blackguard. I'll give you the stick me bucko before you go home today. Now, Master Ryan, why do you think Hillary felt great?'

'Cause he'd done something that nobody else could manage to do. He was a hero, like Ron Delaney when he won the gold medal in Melbourne.'

'Excellent answer, Ryan. He did something heroic; something very special and people all over the world admired him for his achievement. If there were no risks and no danger, then anyone in the world could do it and there would be no hero, nothing to applaud or admire. If Our Lord guaranteed to catch Hillary, or anybody for that matter, should they fall off the mountain, then getting to the top would mean very little.'

'But I don't see anything heroic in babies starving to death,' argued Patsy, 'or dying in an earthquake. And even worse, Sir, how could Jesus let those Nazis put the Jews in the gas chambers?'

'Don't forget the Jews crucified Our Lord,' said Noel Browne.

'Why don't you shut your fuc...!'

'Fagan!' the teacher shouted, before Patsy finished the sentence. 'I think, Browne, you should keep your obnoxious opinions about whether the Jews deserved to be put in the gas chambers or not to yourself. Do you hear me clearly?'

'Yes, Sir,' answered a contrite Browne.

'The world is not a perfect place, Patsy Fagan, and Jesus does not make airplanes, men do, and men are imperfect and make machines that can go wrong. You should already know that Adam and Eve disobeyed God in the Garden of Eden, and the Paradise that God had made for them changed forever. God told them the world would be a hard place to live in, and after their sin—original sin—people would have to work hard and would feel pain and suffering and so on. But God left us with freewill where we could choose.'

'But children don't choose to starve or Jews to go into the gas chamber, Sir,' protested Patsy.

'Between good and evil,' replied Mr Bambrick, 'free to choose between good and evil. The Nazis chose to do a great deal of evil and millions of people suffered. Would you rather that God took away from us the freedom to choose? That people behaved like sheep or robots, controlled by God, acting like clockwork soldiers. You just wind them up and they move according to the way they were made. Do you think, Master Fagan, that people should not be able to choose?'

'No, Sir, I think they should be able to choose but not choose evil.'

'Then they cannot choose good either, because if they are not allowed to choose to be evil, they are controlled like the robots we mentioned and can only act in a certain way. But don't forget, boys, there are many great men and women who fight against evil, who choose good and who often risk their lives to help others who have been persecuted and hounded. Some of you might even be able to find out about people who opposed what the Nazis were doing in Germany and France and Holland and other countries, some of them even put to death by the Nazis.'

'That still doesn't explain why God lets earthquakes happen,' said Patsy.

'Well, I explained that after Original Sin, the earth was a hard place to live in. There are natural physical laws that allow for winter, spring, summer and autumn seasons to come around every year. Natural laws cause sunshine and storms, thunder and lighting, flooding, volcanoes and earthquakes, and innocent people can die in all these conditions. Droughts and famines happen and people die.

'But just like people fighting against evil in the world, people can be heroic in coming to the rescue of others, helping them feed the hungry in Africa and India. Doctors and nurses go to countries where there have been natural disasters and do great work, noble work. And even we can help when we put our pennies in the collection boxes.'

The pupils and teacher continued to explore all the "buts and what ifs" and all the "but that isn't the same" until the afternoon came to an end and the bell was rung for the end of the school day. Reddy Costello duly received four strokes on each hand, making a determined effort not to show any fear or pain as the bamboo swished through the air leaving angry red welts on the palm of the boy's hand. As he, Patsy and Gurky made their way home together, Gurky remarked, 'I'll tell you what, Reddy.'

'What?'

'You were a shaggin hero the way you took that stick from aul Bambo.'

Chapter 12

Patsy had a school holiday job in Mr Howard's butcher's shop in Cabra. The Howards lived in Landscape Avenue and Patsy went each morning with Mr Howard in his Ford van, full of sleep and wishing his father had found him a job nearer home.

He found working in a butcher's shop a cold occupation, whether it was emptying the large chiller every day to fill up the windows with rashers, sausages, pigs' trotters, ox tail, liver, kidneys, lambs' hearts and heads, ox tongue and sweetbreads, or dipping his hands and arms up to the shoulders into the forty-gallon stainless steel barrel of brine at the back of the shop to drag out the large joints of silverside or brisket that had been pickling for up to ten days. His hands and arms would feel numb with cold after ten minutes and the colour of them often frightened him.

They resembled the pale bluish shells of mussels, not yet matured, that you found clinging to the rocks in Dalkey, after the tide had gone out. He was afraid his hands and arms would take on a permanent dye and the watery sheen from the brine barrel would cause his skin to remain wrinkled, as when someone has stayed in a bath for too long.

His principal duty was to ride the heavy messenger-bike, delivering the meat and poultry to Mr Howard's customers, some living as much as three miles from the shop. Orders for meat came by phone or letter but more often than not it was ordered during the weekly visit to the shop by the customers themselves when they came shopping, usually on a Friday afternoon or a Saturday morning.

Mr Howard's order book had a page for each customer and the separate requirements for Mondays, Tuesdays, Wednesdays and so on, were meticulously entered. The best time for delivery was also recorded, along with brief "special instructions" which might read: "Don't frighten the cat", or "Use the side gate", or "If not in, leave next door". One customer always said, "Bring change of a £1 note." Mr Howard insisted that all customers' "little idiosyncrasies" were to be fully respected.

When he delivered "dry" parcels such as sausages, puddings, steaks, chops and dripping, Patsy used the large wickerwork basket that sat in the black tubular steel cradle on the front of the messenger bike. An old bicycle tyre had been cut and fitted to the curled-over top perimeter of the basket to protect it from being damaged when laid roughly against garden walls made of stone or brick, or worst of all, pebble-dashed blocks of which there were many in the Cabra area of Dublin.

'Money doesn't grow on trees,' Mr Howard was fond of saying. 'For crying out loud, be careful with the bike, Patsy, and don't bash that basket against the walls the way the bowsie in Murphy's does.'

'Ok, Mr Howard.'

Patsy liked the messenger-boy in Murphy's grocery shop and the way he handled his heavily laden bike, skimming walls and rails, jumping curbs and footpaths and riding through the narrowest of side-entrance passageways, parking his machine as close to the point of delivery as possible.

'How are you, Sean?' Patsy called as both boys were leaving their shops with full baskets.

'Ah, grand thanks, Patsy, and yourself?'

'I'm fine, Sean. Any chance of showing me how you jump the bike over that big kerb by Doyle's Corner?'

'Of course! It's dead easy. I'll be down there in about fifteen minutes. Will you be anywhere near?'

'Yeah, I'll make sure I am. See you.'

Like other messenger-boys, he became skilled in the art of handling a heavy and cumbersome bicycle, knowing how to shift his own weight on the saddle of the bike to counterbalance the weight in the basket at the front. Often it was an uneven contest and the overfull basket won the day. Boy and meat were scattered across a road or dumped onto the driveway of a house, sausages and black and white puddings bursting from their white paper wrappings and rolling in their fine greaseproof paper to mix with dirt and gravel.

Patsy, knees and arms grazed, cursing and damning everything in sight, would pick himself up and start the job of gathering his goods, examining each item, cleaning it as necessary with his white apron and re-wrapping it in what he hoped was its original piece of white paper. The worst incidents were those when he was bleeding from the fall and his blood got onto the meat when he was rearranging it, or when the sausages or puddings had broken into pieces and burst their skins. He knew to expect trouble when he heard a customer in the shop complaining.

'It's no good sending me white pudding that looks like it's been through the mincer, Mr Howard, and sausages with the skins burst and the meat in them sticking all over the paper and all. And I found bits of stone and grass in the half pound of minced meat.'

Patsy expected Mr Howard's attention as soon as the customer had left the shop with "free" sausages and pudding.

'Didn't I tell you to be careful with the bike, and not to be messing about with that little ballocks from Murphy's doing all the fancy tricks. I hear all about it, don't you worry me bucko, from Mr Connolly down at Doyle's Corner. If I hear of any further conniving with that gurrier, I'll take the arse off you. Do you hear me, Patsy Fagan?'

On Tuesdays, Patsy put the aluminium "basket" in the bike's cradle to go to the abattoir in Phibsboro to collect the offal that Mr Howard had ordered for the week. His cousin, Billy O'Hara, was working there as a tea-boy and doing general cleaning up.

'C'mon and I'll show you round the place,' he said when Patsy first visited.

Patsy was not expecting the overpowering smell of urine and animal waste and what he knew to be blood when Billy led him into the huge main slaughtering shed. At one end, cattle were kept in enclosed pens with perhaps ten to fifteen beasts in each pen. Billy knew all the butchers and the apprentice butchers and introduced his cousin.

'How do yous kill them?' Patsy asked.

'Ah, it's very quick,' answered one of the apprentices. 'You shoot them in the head with this and they're dead instantly.'

He lifted a very large, revolver-shaped, stainless-steel gun, the like of which Patsy had never seen before, not even in the pictures, but unmistakably a gun just the same.

'What sort of bullets does it fire?' he asked.

'They're not bullets,' the apprentice answered, 'It's this skewer thing.'

Patsy looked, feeling a little sick in his stomach, at the ten-inch steel needle, twisted in the shape of a corkscrew, quarter an inch in diameter, one end sharply pointed like a pencil, with a two-foot steel wire hanging loose attached to the flat end.

'What's that wire for and how do you shoot it?' Patsy asked.

'You put the skewer in when you open up the gun like this.'

The apprentice used both hands and a knee for leverage, to break the gun. He opened it fully and pushed the needle into the barrel from the rear end and slid it all the way in until only the length of thin gauge wire was hanging out. He closed the gun with a loud snap, drawing the steel wire through a tiny aperture on the top of the gun, thus allowing the wire to pass through and follow the needle to which it was attached when the gun was fired.

'They're going to be slaughtering in a few minutes,' said the apprentice. 'Billy'll slip you down so you can have a look for yourself.'

They went to the end of the pens to another enclosed pen that was smaller than the others and which held only one animal. The floor was made of concrete and had a tiled trough about six inches wide running the length of the pen. There were smaller channels cut into the concrete floor, which ran into the tiled trough. The pens were connected to each other and animals could pass from one pen to the next through a steel barred gate that the herdsman would open.

As Patsy and Billy arrived, a single animal was being herded through the gate into the small killing pen. The beast was full of fear and panic, its eyes rolling wildly; it had already emptied itself of urine and excrement in the holding pens.

The butcher stepped onto the lowest rail of the pen fence, leant over the top rail as far as he could and placed the barrel of the gun hard against the cow's forehead and fired. He did it so quickly that the cow had not even time to move its head away. The noise was deafening and Patsy stood there stunned, almost wetting himself. He looked at the shot beast which was still standing, and then suddenly it fell, as if an enormous hand had knocked its legs away with a single blow.

The cow did not crumple to the floor but rather dropped with a frightening thud as if it had been thrown from a high building. The butcher had entered the pen and took hold of the length of wire that was protruding from the unfortunate beast's head and was retrieving the steel needle which had penetrated skull and brain. He cut the animal's throat and dragged its head as near to the tiled trough as he could so that the blood ran freely in the duct to be collected in large vats.

'What did you think?' Billy asked when the two went outside to share a cigarette.

'I was nearly feckin sick,' answered Patsy.

'Wait'll you see the sheep. That'll make you feel real bad. We all grab a sheep, me and all, and we hold them over a huge long gutter, half the length of the shed. Then the butcher comes along and lifts the sheep's head with one hand and cuts its throat with the other. He does a load of sheep at the one time and only stops to sharpen his knife. When he's done your sheep, you lay it on the floor with its head in the gutter to let the blood flow and not mess up the place.

'Sometimes it makes you fuckin sick when you see them kicking their legs and everything. You wonder if they're in much pain and all.'

'I don't think I want to see the sheep been done,' said Patsy. 'I suppose you have to be cruel to do this work all the time. I'm glad I don't have to do it.'

'Course, you don't have to be cruel,' said an offended Billy. 'I'm going to see if they'll start me as an apprentice even though I'm a bit older than some of them. I'd do it like the best butchers, quick and all the time talking to the animals, telling them not to be afraid and that it won't hurt and it'll be all over in a few seconds, and think what it'll be like when someone is really enjoying their dinner because of them. I won't be like those two cruel fuckers from Cavan though.'

'What two?' Patsy asked.

'Two feckin gobshite brothers. They're in the last year of their apprenticeship and you should see them when they're herding the cows through the pens, sticking their knives into the cows' arses, and they thinking it's great fun. I'm telling you, knives right in up to three or four inches in the arse or side, and the poor shaggin cows screaming and crying with the pain, shitting and pissing all over the place, and worse still, I've got to go and clean it fuckin up. I'd like to do those two ignorant bastards.'

When Patsy went to the abattoir the following Tuesday, he was met by his cousin, Billy.

'I want to show you something,' he said, nodding his head for Patsy to follow him.

He led Patsy along a pathway to the back of the main shed where the abattoir workers parked their cars and bikes.

'Be careful now,' said Billy. 'I don't want to be seen. I heard the two culchies from Cavan talking this morning, saying their Da lent them his brand new car, would you believe, to go flashy all over Dublin, our city I ask you, and they was to bring it back home next weekend without a single mark on it and all. I think meself it's fuckin gas.'

'What is?' Patsy asked.

'Sneak down between them cars and vans. You can't miss it. It's a Ford Consul. Go on quick.'

Patsy bent low and skipped between the cars until he spotted a two-tone blue and white Mark 2 Ford Consul, immaculately clean and obviously new. He could see nothing remarkable until he was almost on top of the car. A side window of the passenger rear door had been smashed, and when Patsy looked in, he found a large load of animal sewerage from pigs, cattle and sheep had been spread all over the inside of the car. Bucket loads of every sort of offal and blood were staining every piece of fabric.

Portions of liver and tripe were stuffed into ashtrays, heater vents, glove compartment and door pockets. And there, the *piece de resistance*, perched on the driver's seat staring at you as you opened the door, was the decapitated head of a cow, horns still in place, tongue sticking out the side of the mouth, big brown eyes, dulled now, and a large sheet of butcher's wrapping paper impaled on the horns with a message scrawled in animal blood on it, which read: REVENGE OF THE COWS, YOUS TWO DIRTY FUCKIN CULCHIE BALLOCKSES.

'When you deliver the corned beef to Mrs Burke in number 35, go next door and knock on Mrs Abraham's door. She wants to make an order and don't make too much noise. She likes you to speak softly, do you hear, Patsy, are you listening?'

'Course I am, Mr Howard,' answered Patsy, putting on his bicycle clips to protect the legs of his new "longers".

Patsy did as he was told and knocked on Mrs Abraham's door but there was no answer so he knocked again, harder this time. On the third knock, an upstairs window opened and Mrs Abraham stuck her head out the window.

'Yes, what is it? I'm just got out of the bath. Could you not be a bit more patient. What do you want?'

'I'm sorry, Missis, but Mr Howard told me to knock and get your order. I've got a notebook and pencil with me.'

'Oh for goodness sake, I'm not dressed. I can't come down to the door. Can you come back this afternoon?'

'I don't know, Missis, I usually have to do the corn beef pickling on Wednesdays.'

'All right then, I'll call it down to you. Come on up on the lawn nearer to the window.'

Patsy climbed over the low box hedge and went across the lawn until he was beneath the upstairs bedroom window.

'Right,' said Mrs Abraham, lowering her voice, 'two pork chops with the kidneys left on them and a pound of pork sausages.'

'I'm sorry, Missis, I couldn't hear you,' said Patsy. 'Could you repeat that please.'

'Keep your voice down. Are you ready?'

'Yes,' Patsy whispered.

'Two pork chops with the kidneys left on them and a pound of pork sausages. Have you got that, young fella?'

'I have Missis,' answered Patsy, turning towards the garden gate.

Just before he reached the messenger bike, he turned and saw Mrs Abraham in the act of closing her bedroom window and he called out in a good strong voice: 'Excuse me, Missis; did you want the fat left on the pork chops or do you want them trimmed?'

'Would you keep your bloody voice down!' Mrs Abraham whispered as loudly as she possibly could.

Next day, after Patsy had made his early round on the bike, Mr Howard called him out to the back of the shop.

'What sort of a little ballocks are you?'

'What's up, what did I do wrong?'

'Didn't I tell you to keep your gob shut and not to make noise when you went to Mrs Abraham?'

'Yeah, but I had to find out whether she wanted the pork chops with fat on or with them trimmed. You always tell me to find out and give out to me if I forget.'

'Forget me arsehole. Mrs Abraham is Jewish, you feckin eegit.'

I felt an awful fool of course, but then Mr Howard should've told me about her been Jewish and all. Mind you, I'm not sure I'd have caught on about the pork. It's not something that comes into me mind if I think about Jews or Mohammedans or Catholics. What food they eat or are not allowed to eat. Well, I do think about it when it's Friday and you can't eat meat, but everyone knows it's a fast day and Catholics have to eat fish.

"Best meal of the week," that's what Da says. "You can't do better than a nice mackerel or a piece of haddock, fresh out of the sea." Not everybody knows about it just the same. Tony says in England, they can have meat any day and they don't always bother about fish on Fridays. He says lots of Catholics in Coventry eat meat on Fridays and our cousins think it's great gas that we're still backward with all those silly rules and superstitions.

He says some Catholics over there never go to Mass, and when all the Irish fellas and girls arrive in England, looking for work and all, the first visit they get in their lodging houses is from the parish priest to make sure they go to Mass and confession. Da said the priests in Ireland only visit if they want money or some free work done to the church, or when they're looking for a ton of logs for nothing.

The Irish girls in England are better than the fellas at getting up on Sunday morning to go to the church, Tony says. The men in the pub tell each other how they promised their Ma they would never miss a Sunday, but with only a few weeks gone by, a lot of them don't go, or they turn up at the end of Mass and pretend to their friends and the priest they've been there all the time, and then they go off to the pub together.

He's really enjoying England but we miss him. I think Ma would really love him to come back for good. Da says what's the use of that and we might all be joining him over there sooner rather than later if the government here doesn't get up off its arse and do something for the working man. I'd like to go and see for meself what it's like over there, although Tony says I wouldn't like the food, and Irish food is better.

I wonder if our pork chops with the kidneys left on are better. Jesus, he was fuming aul Howard, miserable ballocks. Food and religion, funny really when you think about it. They always seem to go together. Jesus turning the water into great wine at the wedding and feeding millions of people who were starving with just a handful of loaves and fishes. And He was drinking wine with tax collectors and old whores and telling parables about feasts and parties.

I never understand the one where the younger son comes home after he's been a waster and spending all the money his Da gave him, and they all make a fuss over him, especially his da. You'd imagine he'd get a good hiding after all the trouble he'd been, but instead, they got the best calf and slaughtered it (I wonder how they killed it) and had a great party and all to celebrate the son's return. But what choice did the son have except to return and beg off his da?

He was broke and wasn't able to get a good job, so he was glad to get back home. Mr Bambrick said you couldn't understand the parable properly unless you were a Da yourself.

The older son wasn't all that pleased either; he probably didn't like to see the best calf going to feed the brother who'd already had his share of his da's fortune and was now digging into his share. You can't really blame the older fella for been put out a bit.

Then there's the last supper, that's the most important meal Jesus had with the disciples, I suppose, which you can understand seen as it was His last meal. That's where the Mass was invented, when Jesus broke the bread and gave it to them telling them it was His body and they had to eat it. It's strange really when you think about it because we're taught that the bread or host as we call it is the very real body of Jesus.

It's not pretending or letting on but as that cow Sister Agnes used to say, "It's the living flesh of Jesus". Not even the dead flesh you'll notice but the "living flesh" and we have to eat it. What does that make the disciples and us? Cannibals if we're honest, and not ordinary everyday cannibals that eat dead people, but real, right bowsie cannibals that eat "living flesh", fresh off the body how are you.

Accipite et manducate ex hoc omnes. *Take and eat you all of this.* Hoc est enim Corpus meum. *For this is my body.*

It's from all the "hocs" "hics" and "huncs" that we got the saying "hocus pocus". The Mass is the feast when all the Catholics come together on Sundays and holy days of obligation to eat the body of Jesus and drink His blood. If you were telling that to somebody from another planet who'd never heard of Jesus, they'd think you were an awful shaggin savage altogether.

When I took the sausages and chops back to Mrs Abraham, she asked me to come into the kitchen for a minute so she could pay me. I told her I was terribly sorry for embarrassing her in front of the neighbours and all, and she blushed and asked me what I meant. I explained that Mr Howard had told me she was Jewish and that Jews weren't allowed to eat pork and I shouldn't have raised me voice so loud, so that the neighbours would hear.

She blushed even more and said the sausages and chops were for "gentile" friends who were coming for lunch and had a partial fondness for pork. I said that I thought it was silly about food and religion, and I even told her what Tony said about the Catholics in Coventry. She laughed and asked me if I'd like a cup of tea or a glass of lemonade. So there we were in the kitchen like two aul ones chatting away to our hearts' content.

I told her all about Emmet House and Mr Marcus and Robert Emmet. I said Mr Marcus was the only other Jew I ever met and that was only when I was small, but I let her know I knew all about the synagogue that the Nazis had bombed, and that we had talked a great deal of the war in aul Bambo's class and all the awful things that had happened to the Jews.

I told her I had tried to find out as much as I could about people who had helped Jewish people escape the Nazis, and that Mr Bambrick called me "a true Dublin Isaiah". I think she had a tear in her eye and she took out her hankie and gave her nose a huge blow that made her shake all over.

"I want to lend you a book, but you must promise to bring it back to me." Which of course I did, and she put the book in me hands. "It's a truly wonderful book of a young girl who was a true heroine, though she never killed anybody, or did great brave things like your Robert Emmet. But she had the same courage and the same noble thoughts as he." I looked at the title and read the name The Diary of Anne Frank, and I turned over some pages and saw there were a few old photographs in the middle of the book.

One of the photographs was of Anne Frank herself when she was 13, sat at a desk or table with a book in front of her. She had long black hair and very dark eyes, and she was smiling and looking straight at you, and she was wearing a lacy white dress with short sleeves. I noticed she was wearing a wristwatch with a black leather strap. I looked at the picture a long time and there was a tear in my eye as well because she looked like my dead sister, Alana.

Chapter 13

'And why are you not going to Synge St School then?' Reddy Costello asked when they were in the school playground.

'Me Ma said it was something to do with the Christian Brothers not wanting me because me Da doesn't go to Mass every Sunday.'

'I wouldn't stand a fuckin chance then,' answered Reddy. 'My aul fella hasn't been near a church since he got his First Holy Communion money.'

'Yeah, but you're not interested in carrying on, are you? Me Ma is really upset. She had her heart set on Synge St. I think she thought they'd be standing in a line waiting to grab me as I walked in the door.'

'What did your Da have to say?'

'He was shaggin mad. They didn't even ask me to come down for a meeting, which is the least you can expect. Me da's detective friend rang the headmaster cause he's got a son there himself and asked if there was any news of the application me Ma sent in. The headmaster said he was writing to me parents, but the answer was no because me Da was not known in the parish, and the parish priest couldn't recommend me on account of it.'

'Fuckin unholy ballocks,' observed Reddy Costello.

'What's the matter with yous two?' Gurky Ryan asked, as he joined them. 'Yis look like you've been to a funeral or you've missed your tea.'

'They won't take Patsy in Synge St after all,' answered Reddy.

'Jaysus, you're feckin lucky,' said Gurky. 'So you don't have to carry on after all.'

'I want to carry on, for Christ's sake,' answered Patsy and carried on explaining to Reddy: 'Me Da doesn't believe it's because he doesn't go to Mass every Sunday. He says they give first places to culchies and they don't give a shite about Dublin lads. I think though he's blaming himself for not going to Mass.'

'He's right,' said Gurky. 'When I told me Da you was going there, he said good luck to you, but you weren't a farmer's son and your Da wasn't a policeman, and you didn't have an uncle for a priest, as far as he knew, and so why would they be giving a place to a poor jackeen like yourself in the first place.'

'So now what's going to happen?' Reddy asked.

'A friend of me Da told him there was a school near Landsdowne Rd where they play the rugby…'

'Awful bloody savage game that. They should be all locked up,' interrupted Reddy.

'…Which has a good reputation,' continued Patsy, 'and me Ma has to make an appointment with the headmaster to take me down there to meet him.'

In the warm Easter sunshine, Patsy made his way to his father's garage when he got out of school at 3 o'clock. He often went and spent two or three hours helping out around the place, either doing a little sweeping and cleaning, or wiping the car windscreens with a clean chamois leather and a bucket of cold water. Most of all, he enjoyed it when his father asked him to start up the cars to let them run in order to warm the engines and keep the batteries well-charged, 'In case someone comes in and asks if he can hear the engine going. We don't want a flat battery, do we?'

Patsy took the opportunity of putting the different cars into gear when he had started the engines, engaging each gear without releasing the clutch so that the cars did not move. He was already a competent driver, having learnt the basics on the invalid carriage along with his brother, Tony. His father had taken him into a field a number of times and gave him plenty of practice driving different cars and trucks and vans.

Miss Cooney, who owned a hole-in-the-wall grocery shop near Landscape Avenue, asked him nearly every Friday to deliver grocery orders to customers. Some lived as much as four or five miles from the shop, too far for a heavy load on the ancient messenger bike. She trusted Patsy to take her blue 5 CWT Fordson Van, loaded to the hilt with every sort of vegetable, packet, tins and bottles. She put several cushions on the seat so Patsy could see over the top of the steering wheel, and off he went, no driving licence and no insurance.

'A blind man can get a driving licence in Ireland,' his uncle Michael said. 'It's a damn disgrace, it is, when you see the bowsies driving on the roads and not an ounce of intelligence between them, and yet they give them driving licences. I wouldn't let them take charge of a donkey and ass. They wouldn't do it in England. By Jesus, they wouldn't. They'd have to take a test there and I can't imagine even a single one of them passing a tenth of it. Driving by Christ. Driving you feckin mad is more like it.'

Tom Fagan had been in the small garage for two months. He had taken the difficult decision to give up his timber and turf business but he had recognised the preferences his customers were making. The spread of central heating in Dublin, fuelled by coal burning boilers or, in many cases gas, spelt the end of open fires, and all the dirt they caused, and the daily emptying of ashes and cleaning that went with them. It had been a painful time for Tom Fagan.

He knew most of his regular customers since his boyhood in the early 1920s. He had looked after them well and when times had been tough, as during the war, with fuel rationing, he had managed to keep them going. They had appreciated him and many were very fond of him, and thought of him in much the same way they did a favourite servant. They knew when his wife was expecting another child and would send a gift for the newly born, and he was invited to help himself to flowers from the garden to take to his wife.

At Christmas they gave him a ham or turkey, an occasional goose or duck, and he would come home laden with Christmas pudding and cake to the delight of his young family. He did not want to change his way of living but he sensed the economic dangers that waited for him if he delayed the decision any longer.

He had always been involved with motorcars in some way or other. In the late 1940s and early 50s, he had traded in vans and trucks as well as tending his turf and timber business. He knew how motorcars worked and he had considerable knowledge and skills when they needed repairing. All in all, he felt he was the ideal man to open a small car sales garage, and when he found a garage for rent, though it would have been better described as a yard with a covered area and office in a lane off Westland Row in the centre of Dublin, he believed that the gods were smiling on him.

Indeed, business was good and there was a steady turnover of stock. He bought well either from auctions or from other dealers he had got to know in Dublin. He had contacts in the country and some good friends in Galway and Cork who let him know when there were bargains to be had, and he was not slow to act on such information. To put it mildly, he was feeling satisfied he had made the right decision to put all his capital into his new business.

His "staff" consisted of one, a friend of many years, who had few specific professional or trade skills but could turn his hand to most things and, very importantly, was "good" with people. His name was Charles O'Connor but was known universally as "Nasty" O'Connor. Nobody knew how he had earned this appellation and everybody who knew him would say, if asked, that he was the least objectionable person in the whole of Dublin.

Yet his friends and relations called him "Nasty" and introduced him as such to others. He, himself, answered happily to the name and never considered it to be in any way inappropriate. Had he been married, there is no doubt his wife would have addressed him along with everyone else as "Nasty".

Nasty O'Connor was short and portly and his head was almost entirely hairless; he possessed not a single whisker, nor any sign of an eyebrow and only a tiny hint of blond eyelashes. He was untroubled by nasal hair and his ears were pink, flawless hollows, as devoid of vegetation as the most barren desert on the planet. He had undoubtedly the most cherubic face this side of paradise—rosy cheeked, dimpled chin and big, laughing, happy eyes.

And indeed, Nasty was always happy, or so it seemed, and those who speculated about the nature of his name, concluded wisely, no doubt, that he needed some personal characteristic to stop people believing he was an angel in human flesh, and hence, "Nasty".

Patsy and Nasty got on very well together and Nasty looked forward to Patsy's stints in his father's garage. They cleaned the cars together and polished the coachwork and touched up marks and scratches on the bodywork with small tins of car paint that Tom Fagan provided. They checked the levels of oil, water and brake hydraulic fluid in each car weekly and took care that all cars were ready to be "tested" should a possible customer enter the premises.

When Patsy's father was out buying a car or taking a car to a potential buyer, Nasty allowed Patsy to "move the cars around". They rearranged the positions of the dozen or so cars every few days to give the impression that new cars were being bought and sold all the time. Patsy loved this practice as it gave him the chance to try different gearboxes and clutches and feel the ease that powered steering gave in turning the front wheels of the two or three heavy American motor cars that his father kept in his stock in the hope of attracting Dublin taxi drivers looking for a change of car.

Nasty would stand by, keeping an eye out for Tom Fagan, and at the same time give directions to Patsy manoeuvring the cars around in the tight space, praying silently that the boy would not allow his foot to slip off the clutch, with possible disastrous consequences. It was not that Tom Fagan minded his son driving—he encouraged it—but the shifting and parking of cars in the confined area required experience and skill, and Tom Fagan was unwilling for Patsy to gain such an experience in circumstances which could well cost him money he could ill afford.

Patsy loved the different smells of the cars. He believed he could tell which car he was sat in simply by its smell. He knew the Triumph Mayflower (razor-edge coachwork), "the poor man's Rolls Royce" Nasty called it, by its sweet-smelling cream leather seats. Its previous owner had polished the rich leather interior every week with a mixture of beeswax and turpentine in the belief that it preserved the seats in the best possible condition.

'It certainly gives them a peculiar smell all right,' observed Nasty O'Connor.

'That's my favourite,' said Patsy, pointing to the 1953 Dodge Coronet.

'Ah, sure that car would kill you,' answered Nasty. 'It's got an engine like the Queen Mary.'

And they lifted the bonnet again and looked at the "Red Ram" Hemi V8 engine, Nasty pointing out the carburettor and distributor, and explaining to Patsy what each part did and its relation to the other parts.

'Can you imagine,' asked Nasty, '140 horsepower pushing two ton of steel over a hundred miles an hour.'

'Have you ever done a hundred miles an hour, Nasty?'

'Of course I have, many a time when your dad and I went down to Kilkenny or Wexford, and we got a good stretch of road, your dad would put his foot down and let it rip. It was great gas. Mind you, he always had smashing cars that could do it and stop fast when you needed them to. He had a lovely Frazer Nash when you and Tony were babies that could do a hundred easily.

'It was the first time I ever did it, when he let me drive it from Howth. As we were coming along the North Strand, there was nothing on the road and he said to go on and stick me foot down, and I did. Jesus, Mary and Joseph, I thought we were going to take off for the moon. Your dad was shouting out the speed, "Eighty-five, go on, Nasty! Ninety, ninety-five".

'I didn't dare take me eyes off the road to look at the speedometer. I was glued to the windscreen and your dad excited and shouting, "Ninety-six, seven, eighty, go on! hundred!" I couldn't drive all the way home. I had to get out and have a pee, God forgive me bad language, and let your dad take over.'

'I remember the Studebaker he had when we lived in Emmet House,' said Patsy.

'Do you remember it really? Your dad bought it straight off the docks in Dublin, still in its wooden crate, £1200 he paid, all in £5 notes. A beautiful car, light blue and perfect lines, and just the right amount of chrome.'

'Yeah, I remember. We went on holidays in it to the country, didn't we?'

'You're perfectly right. There was your mam and dad, and the quare fella Dinny was the baby. You were only 4 or 5, and Eileen was getting sick in the back of the car, all over poor Tony's face. Jesus, Mary and Joseph, he thought he was destroyed forever, and then Dinny did a shite on his lap, God forgive me bad language, but poor Tony was cursing and swearing, and your mam took him to a little stream at the side of the road and gave him a good wash in the freezing water.

'She got the baby sick off his face and Dinny's shite off his legs and lap, and she washed his trousers in the stream, the little short corduroys, you know, and she tied them to the car bumper, and poor old Tony had to wrap a towel around him until the trousers dried in the wind.'

'I remember we went a very long way and we arrived in the dark. We could hear the waves coming in off the sea.'

'But how could you?' Nasty asked. 'Sure you were only a little fella. But you're right enough. The seven of us left Harold's Cross about 6 in the morning in that lovely Studebaker—your dad was so proud of it—and the weather was gorgeous. We took the road out to Lucan and then went on to Maynooth. We stopped at a place in the village of Kinnegad, called Harry's, to have sausages and rashers. Jesus, I can still lick the taste on me lips, and then we were off again.'

'I do remember,' said an excited Patsy. 'We went into a big town called Athlone, beside the River Shannon. It was the first time I ever saw the Shannon. And there were lots of soldiers around. Da always called them "Free State Squaddies".'

'He did indeed. It's a town I don't know well and have always found a little strange, though you couldn't find nicer people anywhere. Where were we?'

'In Athlone on our way in the Studebaker,' answered Patsy.

'So we were, and after Athlone, we travelled on to Ballinasloe and then to Loughrea where your uncle Michael was born. And so we had to stop there and see the cranky old shagger, God forgive me bad language, and then at last the jewel of the west, Galway City. Now by Jesus and His Holy Mother, that's a town I love.'

'I can't remember Galway City at all,' said Patsy. 'Are you sure we went there?'

'Am I sure we went there? Sure, where else would you go if you want to get to Connemara and Clifden? Right into the centre of the city and stopped in Eyre Square. Your mam took yous lot for a picnic on the grass and your dad and I went for a pint in the Great Southern Hotel. I can nearly still taste it, God calm me thirst, and they say the Guinness doesn't travel well, but I'll tell you now, the pint in the Great Southern is one of the great pints in the world.'

'I don't know about the pints,' Patsy answered, 'but I'm surprised you like Galway so much. Aren't Dublin men supposed to hate all culchies?'

'Will you go off out of that. That's only Dublin fellas codding. That's the way we talk but we're only joking. Sure, the most reliable men in Ireland come from Galway and other parts of the country too. Your father's best friends are nearly all countrymen.'

'And where did we go on to after Galway City?'

'Well, we stayed in the city for quite a while. All the fellas and their girls out for a walk came over and were looking at the Studebaker. It was brand new, you see, and they hadn't seen the like of it before. They were touching it and feeling the bonnet with the palms of their hands and looking in at the inside. One fella asked if he could sit in it and your dad told him he'd be very welcome.

'Some girls wanted to try the back seat, but your dad said there might be one or two unwelcome deposits left on the seat by the baby, so they didn't bother.'

'But how far further did we have to go? Cause I remember it was dark when we arrived in Uncle Sylvester's and it must've been light in Galway if we were having a picnic.'

'Will you be a little patient? It wasn't all that straight forward, you see. It's fifty miles from Galway City to Clifden, but the road is tiny and twisty and your dad, and even your mam, wanted to stop in some of the little places along the way to say hello to old friends and relations. That's why we were late and didn't get to Clifden until gone midnight. Yous were falling asleep, God forgive us, but we were having great gas.'

Patsy went into the office and returned with a road map of Ireland and opened it up on the bonnet of the Dodge Coronet.

'Show me the way Da went,' he asked.

'There's only one way from Galway City, unless you want to drive out by the Atlantic Ocean. Look, you take this road here all the way along the bottom of Lough Corrib. Now don't forget it's an awful shaggin road, God forgive me bad language, until you come to Oughterard. We stopped there at Keogh's, just for the one pint, mind you.'

'Where were we all the time?' Patsy asked.

'What do you mean, where were you? Yous were all in the car fast asleep and your dad drove it right up against the wall of the pub, so we could listen out for the quare fella crying, or Eileen making a row if she woke up.'

'Was it dark by then?'

'No, not a bit of it. Don't forget it was July, though the sun was going down over Galway Bay. It was a grand sight, and just after you leave Oughterard and follow the river that runs along the road, on your left, for a mile or two, the whole countryside opens up suddenly in front of you, and you can see Connemara stretching way out in the distance and the Twelve Pins standing there with the sun coming through them. And your dad frightening your mam, telling her to watch out, and how they were now in bandit country and she had to look out for Apaches attacking from behind the piles of turf.'

'Show me on the map where that is, and how many miles did we have left?'

'There, look, just about there, and we still had a good thirty miles to go.'

'So we could've still got to Clifden before the sun went down altogether?'

'We could but we made one last stop at a place called Maam Cross, a tiny hamlet with a small hotel. We went in to find a wedding in full fling and wasn't it only a cousin of your uncle Michael that was getting married, a thin, long fella, named Paddy Duane.'

'Uncle Paddy and Nora?'

'The very same, and didn't they force us to stay for the celebrations. Yous woke up and had some milk and lemonade and sandwiches. Your mam and dad were dancing with all the culchies and holding Dinny and Eileen in their arms at the same time. Ah, you should have seen those young fellas and girls at that wedding.

'Tall, dark-skinned lads, black hair, blue eyes and thin and graceful, more like Italians or Spaniards than Irish, and the girls were a match for them, beautiful, by Jesus Christ, they were, may God forgive me taking His holy name in vain.'

During the late spring and early summer of 1958, Patsy and Nasty became great friends, and Patsy learnt as much about the geography of Ireland, outside of Dublin, from Nasty's re-telling of trips and holidays, as he did about Dublin itself, from his walking and cycling, or journeying with his father in truck or van. As their friendship grew, Nasty allowed Patsy more and more latitude in the question of "moving cars" around in the garage. He was willing to let Patsy take the cars "down the lane and turn at the bottom, so you'll be facing in the other direction".

Patsy was careful and managed this exercise without mishap dozens of times, always when his father was out on business. Just as with the fruit in the Garden of Eden, there was one car forbidden.

'Can I take the Dodge today?' Patsy asked.

'No,' replied Nasty.

'Oh come on, you know I'll be alright.'

'No. It's too big for you and too powerful. You'd never see over the top of the steering wheel.'

'I'll put cushions in. I'll be OK.'

'No! The lane's tight enough as it is. Jesus, you give me a heart attack every time I see you turning back into the garage. It's not that wide a gate you know.'

'Please, Nasty, I'll drive real slow.'

'No.'

Patsy persisted whenever he and Nasty were together in the garage and his father was absent.

'Ok,' said Nasty. 'Just the once and no more. Now do you promise?'

'Of course,' replied Patsy. 'Just down to the bottom and then back.'

'I'll be watching you, and if you go fast I'll never let you drive another car.'

'I'll go slow so stop worrying.'

Patsy put some cushions on the seat of the big Dodge Coronet and put the key into the ignition. He pulled the cream bakelite starter knob and listened to the deep growl of the engine. He revved it gently to get the feel of the accelerator on his right foot. When he was ready, he waved to Nasty who was waiting to go outside into the lane to make sure all was clear for Patsy to move out.

Nasty took up his position outside the entrance to the garage and signalled to Patsy to come on. Patsy depressed the clutch and eased the column gearshift into first and let out the clutch gently. The Dodge moved forward and Patsy found it very easy to turn the big car left into the lane as he passed through the red-painted wooden gates of the garage. He nodded to Nasty as he went by and Nasty touched the peak of the tweed cap he was wearing, seemingly praying at the same time.

Patsy drove along the lane slowly and moved into second gear marvelling at the massive power within his control and available instantly at the slightest pressure of his right foot. At the bottom of the lane, he stopped and turned the car by reversing into the open entrance of a small glass-making workshop and then began the journey back up the lane. His confidence grew and he went faster and changed into second gear putting his foot quickly on the accelerator but slowed down again immediately.

He was about a hundred yards from his father's garage and he could see Nasty stood waiting, hands on hips, looking down the lane, immobile…

I was too quick coming back. I'll just reverse back to the end of the lane again and have one more go. He won't be annoyed cause he'll see that it was to do it better the second time.

He reversed the car back to the end of the lane, stopped and shifted into first gear and accelerated quickly; he changed into second and went even faster. The entrance to the garage yard was coming up quickly, too quickly, but Patsy was determined to put the car into third gear before he had finished, which he did, and then immediately braked the car heavily and at the same time began to turn the steering wheel to bring the car back through the garage gates.

He spotted Nasty, standing with his back flat against the outside wall of the garage, with his cap pulled down over his eyes and most of his nose. The big chrome bumper struck the left-hand wooden gate at an angle of about 30 degrees and lifted it off its wrought-iron hinges and propelled it inwards towards the garage office where it came to rest across the bonnet of a Hillman Minx. The Dodge had come to a halt and Patsy got out and immediately went and looked at the front of the big American car to assess the damage.

Apart from a slight grazing to the chrome bumper, there was mercifully very little. Nasty had come to life and now joined him.

'No damage,' Patsy said. 'Do you think if we put the gate back up and clean up the mess, we can tell Da that I was too rough when I was sweeping up and the head of the yard-brush came off and landed on that Hillman Minx?'

'Somehow I don't think he'll believe us, Patsy,' answered Nasty.

Chapter 14

The day for their meeting with the headmaster of Sandymount High School arrived and Patsy and his parents set off from Landscape Avenue in plenty of time for their appointment at 2 o'clock in the afternoon. Patsy was wearing his long grey trousers, white shirt and a tweed jacket that Nasty had given him as a special present "to mark the occasion". He felt smart and clean and he was proud of his parents who looked very "posh and well-turned out", as his mother said.

'There's no need to be afraid or nervous, Patsy. Just relax and answer any questions he asks you as best you can,' advised his father.

'I'm not afraid or nervous.'

'You don't want to be cocky or over-confident either,' added Nuala.

'I'm not feeling cocky or over-confident. I just wish I knew the sorts of questions he's going to ask me.'

What'll I do if I don't know the answer to a question? Should I just say, "I don't the answer to that one, Sir." Or try and bluff and pretend I know something but I'm just having a little difficulty in explaining it. Maybe take Reddy's advice if I'm asked something I don't know. "Just look at the aul ballocks as if he's insulted your intelligence and say to him, 'I couldn't be bothered answering a question like that for Christ's sake, it's too feckin easy.'"

Fat chance I'd get in then. All right for Reddy, and I bet he wouldn't say that anyway, but you never know, he might. Look at the two of them in the front of the car all proud and pleased as punch. I know they can't afford the school fees. Da says if I do well today, they might reduce the cost. Funny that you can barter a bit like you're buying cabbages down in Moore St. "Sixpence a head, lovely Savoys. Go on it's a bargain, Mister. Take two of them home to your missis and she'll love you for it. And you might as well get her some flowers as well."

Da brought home the flowers alright and Ma another baby, a girl. "We'll call her after your sister Rosie," she said to Da.

"Ah, that'll be grand," Da said. "Rosie'll be delighted, especially if we ask her to be the godmother."

She's had eight babies and she's thirty-five years of age. Doesn't seem to bother her and she looks even younger than her age but it must tell on them in the end. They say it's the church's fault in Ireland that the women have so many babies. Tony told me they don't have nearly as many babies in England as they do here.

He said he was right about what he told me when I came to stay with him in Dalkey, about stopping the babies with the little balloons. Why don't we have that in Ireland? Mrs Costello wouldn't have the nine she has now and she the same age as Ma. I wonder if we could ask Mr Bambrick? Don't see why not; it's not as if we're using dirty words or anything, though we couldn't say "dick", but "mickey" would be OK, I'm sure.

Not far now but it'll be a tidy trip in the mornings. Still, it'll be easy on my bike and Ma said when the weather is bad, I'll be able to catch a bus easy enough. Get off at Ballsbridge—I wonder where they got that name from—and walk down Herbert Park into Landsdowne Rd and go across the railway line, right beside the rugby stadium and then you're in Herbert Rd. Da said they play rugby in Sandymount High School and not soccer. He says soccer is a gentlemen's game played by slags and wasters, and rugby is a hooligans' game played by gentlemen and doctors' sons and all.

I asked him about Gaelic football and hurling and he said Gaelic football was for thick eegits and hurling was for madmen who didn't know any better. I think he's wrong, especially about the hurling. You have to be very fast and skilful if you want to play it well. Any eegit can swipe at the ball and sooner or later hit it, but when you see someone running with the ball, bouncing it on the stick and passing it and then getting it back again, and hitting the ball between the posts to score, you realise what a great game it is.

I didn't really know myself until they showed that film Rooney in the pictures. Reddy, Gurky and me went together to the Princess to see it. Reddy said they used newsreel film of Christy Ring, the famous Cork hurling player, in the scenes where Rooney is supposed to be playing in the final of the All Ireland at Croke Park. It was gas with all the fellas in their shorts and all, going into the pub with their hurling sticks and knocking back the pints, and then a big row breaking out between the two teams and everybody fighting and bashing each other, and when it was all over, kissing and mauling each other like they were all in love.

Still, I like all sport and I don't believe you have to be an eegit to play Gaelic football. Sure, most of our politicians and bishops all played Gaelic games at posh schools.

We're here, so it's "once more onto the breach, dear friends". I wonder if he'll ask me anything about Shakespeare. It doesn't look like a school; I wonder where the classrooms are?

They drove into the driveway of a large Victorian town house in Herbert Rd and parked the car. The house belonged to the headmaster, Mr P Cannon, and it served as the administrative block for the school as well as the private residence of the Cannon family. The school itself had been built in the extensive gardens behind the house and consisted of six classrooms and a number of science rooms with facilities for scientific experiments. It was still a small school at the time but had been designed to allow for growth as pupil numbers grew.

'Mr Cannon will be with you in a moment,' said the maid who showed them into a waiting room.

'It's a lovely house,' Nuala Fagan said nervously.

'It stinks of floor polish,' answered Patsy.

'Shush you,' said Patsy's father. 'Why are you always shaggin smelling things?'

'Tom, your language!' Nuala warned.

'Would you like to come and meet the headmaster,' said the maid returning to the waiting room.

'Come and sit down and I'm pleased to meet you,' said Mr Cannon. 'You sit here, Patsy, so I can get a good look at you.'

I like him at least. He's got a good face on him. How old is he? Maybe 50 or 45; doesn't matter. He speaks really nice, friendly, like he wants to be a friend. The maid said he would see us in his "study". They don't have a "study" for the headmaster in Milltown, just the classroom, and no pictures on the wall like here, and all these bookshelves. I wonder if he's read all those.

'So, what do you like most about school, Patsy Fagan?'

'Well, I get on well with most things, but I'm especially fond of the bits of Shakespeare Mr Welsh does with us. And also the questions we have with Mr Bambrick.'

'Questions, what "questions"?'

'It's one lesson a week when we can discuss any subject we want and ask questions that anyone can answer.'

'And what if nobody volunteers an answer?'

'Then Mr Bambrick usually tries to give about ten different possible answers and tells us to think about them and try and to decide what our own opinions are.'

'Your Mr Bambrick sounds an unusually wise schoolteacher. I should like to meet him. And what sorts of topics do you deal with?'

'Oh everything. What it was like in Ireland during the war. Whether we should play football and all against communist countries. What the Germans did to the Jews. Irish history, books, life on other planets.'

'I think we shall have to introduce something similar into Sandymount,' Mr Cannon replied. 'Now tell me, what is your favourite reading?'

'I love reading parts from Shakespeare's plays; not always *all* the play except for a couple that are me favourites.'

'Which are?'

'*Romeo and Juliet* and *Macbeth*.'

'Why do you like those best?'

'I just think the story in *Romeo and Juliet* is so good. You keep thinking they're going to win in the end, that's the fella and the girl, I mean, like in a good film. They have to fight against all the odds but you know it's going to end up OK and the hero will be all right and everybody will know he's a hero, especially the girl.'

'But it doesn't end up OK in *Romeo and Juliet*, does it?' Mr Cannon asked.

'In a queer sort of way it does,' answered Patsy. 'They love each other. He's won her and he puts himself in great danger for her. They take risks for each other and marry and are together. You know their parents and all are never going to get on and there'd always be rowing and fighting. In a way, dying for each other and not being able to live without the other one is sad but right. I mean the ending is very sad but you feel they're together and that makes it all right.'

'And Macbeth?'

'It's different altogether. All the way through you admire him as the hero somehow or other and you can't stand her, Lady Macbeth I mean. Yeah, but he's really evil. When he says, "I am in blood steeped so far, that should I wade no more. Returning were as tedious as go o'er", you feel your skin crawling all over your body. But you still think he's the hero of the story and you feel sorry for him when he's killed. And you don't go away from the story liking any of the other characters particularly.'

'Do you understand all the language in the plays?'

'No, sometimes I have some problems working out exactly what it means, but the language is probably the thing I like best about Shakespeare.'

'How do you mean?'

'It's the way he says something ordinary but makes it extraordinary, almost magic.'

'Give me an example.'

'Well in *Richard III*, Gloucester, that's really Richard, wants to say he's really vexed; that he's feeling completely fed up with things.'

'And how does he express those feelings?'

'He says, "Now is the winter of our discontent".'

'And that's extraordinary?'

'Yeah, I think so.'

'And another example?'

'In *Hamlet*, the Prince, who's Hamlet of course, wants to say it's a pity that it's a sin to commit suicide, but he doesn't just say it like that; he says, "Or that the everlasting had not fixed his canon 'gainst self-slaughter".'

'Yes, well that's fine for Shakespeare; you've convinced me, young Fagan,' said the headmaster, with a warm, encouraging smile. 'What else do you enjoy reading; tell me what you're reading at the moment?'

'I've just finished reading *The Diary of Anne Frank*.'

'Really? And how did you come across that?'

'A Jewish lady out in Cabra that I deliver meat to on Saturdays lent it to me.'

'He's got a Saturday job with one of our neighbours who's got a butcher's shop in Cabra,' Patsy's father explained, believing the headmaster would never be able to work out for himself how his son came to be delivering meat to a Jewish lady on a Saturday.

'Oh I see,' answered Mr Cannon. 'And tell me how you have found Anne Frank's diary, Patsy Fagan?'

'At first, I was just so shocked a girl her age could write like that. I mean her descriptions of everything seemed to be so real, I thought it had to be written by someone grown up. But after a while, you begin to hear the voice of a girl of 14 or 15, and you hear things that only a young person like that would say. I think it's marvellous.

'It's hard to imagine what it was like to live in that tiny secret place for that length of time all locked up and not been able to go out. I can't imagine it at all. But If I were trapped in a situation like that, I'd be delighted if there was somebody like Anne Frank there with you.'

'Wouldn't we all,' Mr Cannon whispered. 'And you know what happen after the family was captured?'

'Yes, I do, and that was the worst thing I've ever read. It was in the epilogue of the book and told you how the whole lot of them the Franks, van Pels and Fritz Pfeffer were taken to the extermination camp in Auschwitz, and how after some months, Anne and her sister, Margot, were separated from their mother and shifted to another concentration camp called Bergen-Belsen. They caught typhus and Margot fell from her bunk and died, and Anne simply couldn't take any more and she felt broken with Margot's death and her mother's as well, just a few weeks before.

'And she didn't know where her father was or whether he was even alive. So, she lay on her bunk alone and sick and let go of her life and left a world that had treated her very harshly, but it was terribly sad because she had brought so much to everybody else and died so young.'

'Her story is very sad,' said Mr Cannon, 'but she can inspire all of us to learn to deal with one another in much better ways than we have done in the past.'

'Yes, Sir, but I only wish we'd been more part of it.'

'What do you mean? More part of what?'

'Ireland, Sir; I wish we had declared war against Germany in 1939 or at least in 1940.'

'But we were a very weak nation, with no navy or Airforce to talk of, and not even much of an army. We'd only been independent for less than twenty years. Our cities would have been bombed and destroyed and we would have been helpless to prevent it. Would you like to have seen Dublin destroyed?'

'Of course not but...' answered Patsy, not wanting to upset the headmaster, but not knowing how to stop.

'But what?'

'Other cities were destroyed and some rebuilt and millions of people suffered...'

'And many Irish people suffered and died, and many were fighting in the armed services of Britain and America and other countries. Was that not enough?'

'I know there were thousands of Irish people working in the factories and fighting in the war, but it wasn't the same as having the nation at war with Germany, sharing in the suffering and hurt of a whole world at war.'

'What do you mean by the "nation"?'

'Well Sir, Robert Emmet spoke of Ireland taking her place amongst the "nations of the world", and Parnell talked of "the progress of Ireland's nationhood".'

'Yes I know,' answered Mr Cannon, 'but I don't yet understand the point you're making.'

'It's just that the Nazis were so wrong, and persecuting the Jews and invading small countries and torturing and destroying girls like Anne Frank and doing all the worst possible things in the world, that you'd think the Irish government would've thought that was the right time for Ireland to really take her place among the nations of the world and not to stay outside and be neutral.'

There was silence in the study and Patsy's parents sat stiff and still, and worried for their son's prospects after what they saw as his defiance of the headmaster's position on Ireland and neutrality during the Second World War. They hardly heard the conversation continue between Mr Cannon and Patsy which went on for a further twenty minutes, covering Patsy's knowledge of arithmetic, geometry, algebra, chemistry and physics.

Headmaster and aspiring pupil ended their "meeting" by visiting the countries of Africa and South America through the naming of capital cities, highest mountains and volcanoes, longest rivers and any other piece of relevant information that Patsy was able to offer. At last, the ordeal was over and Mr Cannon turned to Tom and Nuala Fagan.

'I shall be delighted to have your son as a student and I expect him to do well. He will have to work hard but I have no doubt he has the capacity to do so. I want him to enjoy his schooling and get a great deal from it.'

'It's strange hearing a headmaster saying "enjoy his schooling",' said Patsy's mother, the beginnings of tears of pride and relief in her eyes.

'Well, it's the philosophy of this school, Mrs Fagan. We want to measure success not only in terms of academic progress, but also in some sense in how much our students look forward to coming into school each day. We want them to feel part of a community that is critical and analytical but which also understands responsibility and is willing to not only enjoy the privileges but to take on the duties that come with being a student in a school that promotes student participation and democracy.'

'I don't think we fully understand all that,' Patsy's mother replied, 'but we'll do all we can to make sure Patsy does his best and will not let us or himself down.'

'I'm sure you will,' answered Mr Cannon, 'and one of the best ways of preparing for coming here next September is to make sure that Patsy continues to work hard at Milltown and carries on reading worthwhile literature. Do you hear me, Patsy Fagan?'

'Yes, Sir.'

'What about paying the fees and them things,' enquired Tom Fagan, feeling he ought to ask something.

'I'll write to you in the next month or so, but I can tell you now that Patsy will qualify for a bursary.'

'What exactly does that mean?'

'We are able to offer reduced fees to students who we believe will bring a little something special with them to the school.'

'That's grand and very decent of you,' said Tom Fagan.

'And does Patsy bring something special to the school?' A beaming Nuala asked.

'He does indeed,' replied the headmaster. 'He brings a pleasing honesty and an ability to argue his beliefs on matters that are not easy and are indeed often very controversial. I look forward to receiving him in September. By the way, we have another youngster from the Landscape area starting in September, a girl by the name of Catherine Sullivan. Do you know her?'

Chapter 15

'You mean they have fellas and girls in the same school and in the same classes?' Reddy Costello asked, almost choking on his own incredulity.

'Certainly,' answered Patsy. 'Though I've got to admit, we didn't know that until the headmaster mentioned Catherine Sullivan.'

'And does your Ma not mind with all those mots and their diddies sticking in your face all day long?' asked Reddy. 'Jaysus, I know I couldn't do any shaggin studies with that all round me.'

'There you go again, the same thing on your mind all the time. I'll just have to learn to control meself, won't I?' Patsy said with a sly grin.

'Well, you won't have too much of a problem as far as that snobby Catherine Sullivan's diddies are concerned, cause she hasn't got any.'

'You're just jealous cause she won't give you the time of day,' answered Patsy, grabbing his friend and putting him into a headlock and choking him until he begged for mercy.

'Lemme go, you ballocks,' squeaked Reddy.

'Not until you say, "Catherine Sullivan is the finest of all her sex and the pride of nature".'

'How the fuck can I remember all that?'

'Say it after me: "Catherine Sullivan..."; say it!'

'Catherine Sullivan,' gasped Reddy.

'...is the finest of all her sex; go on, say it.'

'...is the feckin finest of...'

'No "feckins" or "shaggins" or anything else. Just say it properly,' ordered Patsy squeezing even harder.

'OK, OK; is the finest of all her sex.'

'And the pride of nature,' concluded a triumphant Patsy.

'And the pride of nature,' said Reddy with apparent resignation. 'Who has no feckin diddies,' he added quickly as he escaped Patsy's grip.

'What are yous two up to?' Gurky Ryan asked, joining them.

'Just sorting out Patsy's love life for when he goes to his grand school with that "Amn't I really grand meself?" Catherine Sullivan how are you!'

'Well, maybe yis can help me sort out me own love life,' said a down-in the-mouth Gurky. 'Are yous going to that dance in the De La Salle school Saturday week?'

'Bet your life we are,' answered Patsy. 'What's the matter? What's up? Aren't you going as well?'

'Yeah, I'm going but I was wondering if your sister, Eileen, would go with me?'

'What do you mean?' Reddy demanded. 'You mean will she walk behind you down the road or a hundred yards in front of you or will she sit on the same bus, or even be so generous as to be in the same building as yourself.'

'Don't be such a feckin eegit,' answered Gurky. 'I want her to go as me mot.'

'*As me mot*!' Reddy teased. 'Are you going to get down on one knee and say to the beautiful Eileen Fagan, "Will you go to the dance as me mot?" If I was her, I'd tell you to go and fuck off.'

'That's the trouble,' pleaded Gurky. 'I don't know what to say to her. I was hoping you might ask her for me, Patsy.'

'I don't think she'd do it if I asked her,' said Patsy. 'Why don't you ask Dinny to ask her?'

'I did ask him but he said she thinks I'm a right dozy ballocks and there was more chance of her going to a dance with a werewolf than with me.'

'Don't you believe him,' said Patsy. 'Ok, I'll see what I can do, but I'm not making you any promises.'

'Thanks, Patsy, and who are you going with, Reddy?'

'I've kept meself entirely free, so that I can have a look and pick me choice as I find suitable.'

'In other words, that Geraldine Quinn that lives next door to you turned you down again,' said Patsy.

Patsy knew it was not going to be easy persuading his sister, Eileen, to agree to be Gurky's date for the dance in the school hall. The monthly dances in the school were very popular in the Churchtown and Landscape areas and most of the local youth between the ages of 13 and 18 attended. The music was provided by bands coming from a wide area of south Dublin, usually part-time amateurs, but none the less, often talented and sometimes even gifted.

The formula was always the same: 1950's rock-and-roll mixed with the soft, romantic ballads of the decade, with occasional swing numbers of the "Big Bands" from the 40s and 30s, notably Glenn Miller. The half-hour "interlude" in the middle of the evening allowed younger, local bands and singers the opportunity to strut their stuff, many of them hoping to be "discovered" by the talent scouts they imagined were present in large numbers, incognito of course.

The dances were lively, happy affairs, much in the style of American high schools' prom dances that were so often portrayed in Hollywood films of the era.

Patsy was aware that Eileen was fond of Gurky but would she be able to see him as anything other than one of Patsy's gang whom she had known all her life.

He's not asking her to marry him for Christ's sake, just to go to the dance with him and have a few dances. She doesn't have to be glued to him all night or anything. She can talk to her pals and all, and even have dances with other fellas. She's not engaged to him after all. Just go there through the doors with him and if somebody asks, "Oh how are you, Eileen, who did you come with tonight?"

All she has to say is, "With Gurky Ryan. You know Gurky, don't you? Ah, he's a grand fella really." It's not asking much when you think about it, is it? But I'm not sure she'll do it.

Patsy had planned to visit Mount Jerome Cemetery on the Sunday morning following the conversation with Reddy Costello and Gurky Ryan. He usually went once a month to his sister, Alana's, grave, sometimes with his brother, Dinny, or sister, Eileen, and they would put fresh flowers in the glass vases, having first changed the water at the standpipe nearby. They would stay for ten minutes or so and say their prayers silently, and then leave to visit their grandparents in Clanbrassil Street.

Patsy suggested to Eileen that he ask Catherine Sullivan and Gurky to come with them to the cemetery and afterwards, they could all go to the pictures in the city centre. Eileen was surprisingly agreeable, "so long as you don't want me to hold that eegit's hand or anything" was her only comment. Permissions were obtained from parents to be out for the whole day and part of the evening and pocket money was given to buy entry to the cinema and bus fares.

Tom Fagan gave Patsy an extra ten shillings to buy all four fish and chips and some ice cream. The fish and chips were a rare treat but Tom knew his son and daughter worked hard helping at home and he took the opportunity to reward them when he could afford it.

'I'm going into Harold's Cross on Sunday morning, so I can give yous all a lift to Mount Jerome after you've been to Mass, and after that yous can get the bus or walk,' he said, as he slipped the ten-shilling note to Patsy.

The four youngsters slid into the deep leather bench-seat of the huge Willys Knight station wagon that Tom Fagan had recently bought, with the hope of selling it to an ambitious taxi driver or car-hire firm.

'Can I drive, Da?' Patsy asked.

'By Jaysus, it'll be a while before you can drive something like this, me bucko. Did you tell the fair Catherine what you did to the Dodge and the garage gates? And the Dodge only half the size of this. Did he tell you, Catherine? And you, Gurky? Sweeping up he was, and lo and behold, the head of the brush came off he was working so hard. And didn't the head go flying through the air and smash one of the big red gates right off its hinge and then land on the bonnet of a Hillman Minx making about fifteen dents in it and tearing the paintwork to bits.

'Now that's some brush head. And the other poor aul devil, Nasty Conner, standing there listening to this and so embarrassed he just wanted to sink into the ground and disappear. And here's the bold Patsy, "Can I drive, Da?" And what? Take those enormous shaggin iron gates off the cemetery with me lovely Willys Knight?'

Three teenagers nearly hysterical with laughter and a chastened Patsy got out of Tom Fagan's car at Mount Jerome Cemetery in the warm sunny June morning.

'Take care of them, Patsy, and tell Alana I love her,' said his father.

'I will, Da, and thanks very much indeed.'

They walked through the large main gates and on to the long wooded avenue that leads to the heart of the old cemetery. Catherine was carrying wild primroses and Eileen had a small bunch of cut snow-white lilies to place on Alana's grave.

'This place always gives me the creeps,' said Gurky.

'Why?' Catherine asked. 'I always find it so peaceful to walk through here and sometimes to sit and read under the trees.'

'With all these dead people around? You must be joking.'

'Tony wrote in one of his letters that in England they burn the dead bodies as often as they bury them in the ground,' added Eileen.

'They must be an awful lot of savages to do that,' said Gurky.

'Don't be an eegit,' said Patsy. 'There are many countries where cremation is the normal way of dealing with dead people.'

'What's creation?' Gurky asked.

'*Cremation*,' answered a haughty, self-righteous Patsy, 'is when they burn the dead body in a special oven.'

'And what poor unfortunate eegits have to lift the dead bodies and stuff them into an oven and probably getting the legs and arms and all jammed in the oven doors and then having to pull them back out to free them and push them back in again and the oven getting cold all the time the door is open. That's an awful job altogether.'

'Listen, you complete amadan, the bodies are in coffins just like when you bury them in a grave but instead of putting them in a grave, the coffin is put on a sort of trolley and then it's rolled into the oven when the doors are opened. It only takes seconds and then big gas jets are fired and the coffin and everything is burnt very fast.'

'That's an awful waste of a good coffin when some people can't afford one who want to go into a normal grave like these around here.'

'Would you two stop that disgusting conversation,' ordered Eileen. 'Catherine and me don't want to hear about dead bodies and burning people. Patsy Fagan, you ought to be ashamed of yourself talking like that when you're coming here to visit poor Alana's grave.'

'I bet Patsy knows all about the famous people buried here,' said Catherine, coming to the rescue.

'Go on, Patsy,' urged Gurky. 'Who are they all?'

'I don't know all that many. Most of the very famous Irish people like Parnell and Daniel O'Connell are buried in Glasnevin Cemetery on the north side of the city. All the heroes of the 1916 Uprising are also buried over there.'

'There must be somebody famous buried here,' said Gurky. 'It looks a very old graveyard.'

'It was started in the 1830s,' said Patsy, 'and was owned by the General Cemetery Company of Dublin. It made a lot of profit for the men who bought shares in the company.'

'You mean people made money out of dead people?' Eileen asked.

'Yes, of course. You have to buy your plot of ground and the people who run the place and dig the graves and look after the grounds have to be paid. They don't do it for nothing,' explained Patsy, delighted to show off a little in front of

Catherine Sullivan after the mortification his father had put him through in the car on the way down from Landscape.

'You still haven't said anybody famous, Smarty-Pants,' teased Eileen.

'Well, just down there on the right between those trees, Sir William Wilde is buried.'

'Who's he when he's at home?' Gurky asked.

'The father of Oscar Wilde, you eegit.'

'Don't ask who Oscar Wilde was, Gurky,' pleaded Catherine.

'I'm not that much of a thick you know, but why isn't he buried here if his Da is?'

'He died in Paris,' answered Patsy, 'and is buried there. But John Millington Synge, the playwright, is buried here and there's a big grave that belongs to the Guinness family just over there.'

'Well, that's a family that I do know about and me Da knows a lot about them too.'

They found Alana's grave and the two girls busied themselves with changing the water in the half dozen glass vases while Patsy and Gurky made an effort to "tidy up" the plot by clearing leaves and twigs away from the banked soil of the grave. When they had done as much as could be done, they stood around the grave in an easy silence and said their prayers to themselves. Patsy told his dead sister how much he missed her and also that their Da and Ma sent her all their love and thought about her every day of their lives and knew that one day they would see her again in Heaven.

'She was a gas kid,' said Gurky, breaking the silence. 'And she never complained no matter how many times we spilled her out of her pram. She'd never tell your Ma and Da no matter what we got up to.'

'You're right, Gurky,' answered Eileen. 'And it's good of you to remember.'

'I only knew her a little,' said Catherine, 'but I feel I've known her all my life, I've been told so much about her by my own mother and father.'

'Everybody loved her,' said Patsy, holding back his tears, 'because she made everybody feel really happy when they were with her chatting and laughing. And she never felt sorry for herself even though she was so crippled.'

They left Alana's grave and soon found their high spirits as they wandered through the many acres of the cemetery "spotting famous names". They passed near a large rectangular granite tomb about ten feet high on which stood a carved stone dog with no head.

'I wonder what happened to its head,' said Catherine.

'Well, me Da told me,' answered Patsy, 'that the dog's master woke up one night thinking he'd heard a burglar downstairs. The dog slept at the foot of his master's bed and the two of them, dog and the master with a sword in his hand, crept down the stairs to catch the thief but found nobody. Then the master heard something coming from the cellar and the two of them went down as silent as ghosts to see what it was.

'It was pitch dark down there and when they reached the bottom step, the door behind them slammed closed and they couldn't see a thing. The master ran up to the door but it had jammed and he couldn't open it, and the dog started barking and growling, and the master thought there was somebody else in the cellar and that it must be the robber. He started swiping out with the sword here and there and swinging it everywhere and of course, he couldn't see anything.

'There was nobody else in the house and he couldn't get out of the cellar and it wasn't until years afterwards that they found the two skeletons down there, and the strange thing was that the dog's head had been cut right off and they found the dried blood on the blade of the sword. There was also a message scrawled in pencil on the wall of the cellar explaining what had happened, and it was signed by the master. So they buried the two of them together and built this monument and left the head of the dog off when they finished it.'

'Is that true?' an astonished Gurky asked.

'Will you go way out of that, Gurky Ryan, for God's sake,' Eileen cried out. 'That's just one of our da's aul stories.'

'Yeah, but what happened to the dog's head then?'

'Are there no graves at all belonging to film stars or singers…people that we all know?' Eileen demanded to know.

'Or graves of heroes and heroines who were in love with each other or died for each other, Patsy?' Catherine asked, fully intending to tease a blushing Patsy.

'I don't know about in here but I can show you on the way into town the graves of two people who were in love, or at least she was with him.'

'C'mon then,' said Eileen. 'Show us. Is it far?'

'Take your time, I'll show you when we get there. What do yous want, a five-minute bus ride or a twenty-minute walk?'

'Oh, it's a lovely day,' said Catherine. 'Let's walk.'

They left Mount Jerome and walked alongside the small park in Harold's Cross where the unfortunate Alana had been thrown unceremoniously from her pram so many times. Patsy glanced over the low wall into his old infant school, Marymount, devoid of chattering children on this bright Sunday morning.

'That's where we used to live,' he said as they passed Emmet House in Mount Drummond Avenue.

'I know what Dinny would say if he was here now,' said Gurky.

'Show us the bridge once again where you fell in the canal,' laughed Eileen.

They walked down past Leonard's Corner, and Eileen and Patsy waved as they crossed the turning into Harty Place, hoping their grandparents might see them from the window of their cottage.

'What's that awful smell?' Catherine asked.

'O'Keef's, the knackers' yard,' answered Gurky.

'Why does it stink?'

'Because they boil up all the dead aul horses that have died from old age and disease and things and turn them into glue.'

'You're disgusting, Gurky Ryan,' answered Catherine, squeezing her nose between her fingers.

'Jaysus, you want to be here in the middle of the week and then you can really get the scent,' laughed Gurky. 'Me Da says it's a real genuine Dublin smell.'

'It's definitely that,' said Patsy. 'But there's lots of other smells as well, much nicer than this one. Well, here we are.'

'What…this aul church?' Gurky asked.

'This "aul church" as you put it,' answered Patsy, 'is St Patrick's Cathedral, the biggest church in the whole of Ireland.'

'But we're not allowed in it,' continued Gurky. 'We're Catholics and this is Protestant, isn't it?'

'Whether we're allowed in or not, we're going in,' said Patsy.

'Why is it called St Patrick's if it isn't Catholic?' Eileen asked. 'St Patrick is the patron saint of Ireland and all the Catholics, isn't he?'

'Yes,' replied a patient Patsy. 'When it was built by the Anglo-Normans in the 12th century, it was Catholic, cause there were only Catholics then; there were no Protestants; there were Jews and Mohammedans and all but no Protestants. But when Henry VIII couldn't get married to his next wife because the Pope wouldn't allow him to divorce the other one, then he started what they call the Reformation and he made all the churches in Ireland and England obey him and not the Pope.'

'But we've got Catholic churches in Dublin,' said Gurky, 'loads of them.'

'Yes, that's because in the last century the English rulers allowed the people to be Catholic again and build new churches, but the Protestants kept the ones they already had.'

'But that's the same as stealing the churches from the Catholics,' said Eileen.

'I suppose it could be,' answered Patsy, floundering. 'But the Reformation was about four hundred years ago, so the Protestants think, you know, that it's natural that the older churches are theirs.'

'Where's our Catholic cathedral then?' an indignant Gurky demanded.

'That's the Pro-Cathedral in Marlborough Street,' Catherine answered. 'We learnt in school that "Pro" means "instead of", or "in place of".'

'So we have an "instead of" cathedral,' said Gurky. 'Jaysus, that sounds gas alright.'

'But what about Christchurch Cathedral just up the road?' Eileen asked.

'Da says that's the finest church in all of Dublin.'

'That's also Protestant,' said Catherine. 'Though they don't always say "Protestant", they say "Church of Ireland".'

'But why have we only got an "instead of" cathedral?' Gurky wanted to know.

'Because the Archbishop doesn't know which church he wants as the real cathedral, or whether he wants to build a new one or not,' Catherine answered.

'Well, Jaysus, that's a right state of affairs OK,' said Gurky. 'The Protestants have two aul cathedrals and we haven't even got one, except for that other yoke of an instead of thing. And there's not that many Protestants. I only know the ones from Newcastle in England, living in our street. Can't they not let us have one of them back if we promise to look after it and all.

'I'll bet you one thing, they'd take a lot more money in the collections on a Sunday at Mass if the Catholics was running the show; do yis know what I mean?'

The four walked through the porch into the dark interior of the cathedral as no service was in progress. Catherine and Eileen slipped on the nylon scarves they had worn earlier in the day at Mass in Landscape. Patsy led the way into the nave and headed towards the altar.

'It's really beautiful,' whispered Eileen. 'Look at those lovely tiles on the floor.'

'They're gorgeous alright,' Gurky replied. 'And those big coloured windows are fantastic.'

'Where are the lovers?' Catherine whispered to Patsy.

'I'll show you in a minute but first, I thought yous would all like a look at the cathedral itself. Gurky and Eileen have never been here before.'

'Nor me either,' answered Catherine. 'I do love the darkness and the smell of the wood and candles.'

Patsy was taking great pride in showing his sister and friends the cathedral. He felt he owned the great architecture of Dublin that was accessible to the public, not in terms of proprietorship of walls, rooms, staircases and land, but more as an inheritor of history. This was his city and its great historical buildings and monuments were his legacy and his means of staying in touch with the past.

It was of no consequence to him that a church was Catholic or Protestant, and completely unimportant that Emmet and Parnell had been Anglo-Irish Protestants. What counted for him were the greatness of the person and the grandness of the historical significance of the street or building.

He wanted others to feel the same admiration he felt for the heroes of the past and to stand in awe on the ground and in the buildings where great events had unfolded.

'And can I be of any assistance to you, young ladies and gentlemen?' asked a voice from a dark corner in the north transept.

A small very old man emerged from the shadows. He was wearing a slightly faded cassock that covered his feet entirely and brushed softly on the ceramic tiles. He was very thin, of medium height, with white hair swept straight back; he was wearing steel-framed glasses over sparkling, light blue eyes and he was smiling.

'Thank you, Father,' Catherine replied. 'We've just come in to have a look, and to see the eh…tomb of…'

'Yes, what tomb do you wish to see?'

'I don't know,' said Catherine. 'It was somebody who was in love with somebody else, I think. Patsy Fagan knows. We're following him.'

'Are you really? I think I know who you might mean, but first of all, let me tell you that I'm not a "Father", I haven't got the honour.'

'But you're wearing a priest's clothes, Father, sorry, not Father,' said Gurky Ryan.

'I am indeed dressed in clerical garb because I am a verger in this cathedral church of St Patrick. That means I have to make sure that people are made to feel welcome and the place is warm and there are candles for the services and so on and so on. But right now, I'm delighted to be at your service and tell you anything you want to know about our lovely church.'

'Where did all them flags come from?' Gurky asked, pointing to a number of standards and military ensigns hanging from poles jutting out of the inner wall of the north transept.

'They came from army regiments that fought in various campaigns in different wars up to when we became an independent nation. Look, this one was held by some soldier leading an Irish regiment into a battle during the Boer War.'

'They look very old and delicate,' said Catherine.

'There's a Union Jack up there,' said Gurky. 'How's there an English flag here?'

'These were the symbols of the British Empire of which we were part. The Boer War and Trafalgar and Waterloo, and even the First World War are all part of the History of Ireland as much as they are of the other countries of the empire. Irish regiments and Irishmen have fought in all the major battles on land and at sea for the last two hundred years and more.'

'Jaysus, I never knew that,' said Gurky.

'And some of the greatest leaders in the history of the empire were born in Ireland. You have the Duke of Wellington and Lord Kitchener, just to name two of many, and even in the last war you had Field Marshall General Montgomery whose family had lived in Ireland for centuries. Where better a place than here in the heart of Old Dublin to cherish their memories?'

'Isn't that great?' whispered Gurky to Eileen. 'Will you go to the dance with me next Saturday?'

'Shush,' Eileen whispered back.

'But you haven't come here to hear me rattling on about old soldiers.'

'You've come to hear about…what was it you said, young woman? "Somebody who was in love with somebody". Follow me and I'll show you what you came to see.'

They fell in behind the ancient verger and followed him across the nave into the south aisle back towards the porch. Eileen took hold of Gurky's jacket and drew him back a little.

'I'll go with you if you promise me not to be trying to maul me or hug me or anything.'

'What about just trying to give you a little kiss?' Gurky asked.

'Jesus, I'll bite the lips off your face if try that.'

The old man stopped a few yards short of the exit and the four visitors gathered around him.

'Look,' he said, pointing to the floor. 'Here's where they are buried, side by side. Jonathan Swift and Stella. Do you want to hear the romantic version or just historical facts?'

'The romantic!' Catherine and Eileen chimed together.

'Well, he met her in England and when he returned to Dublin as Dean of this great cathedral, she followed him, so much was she in love with him. Some think she was his cousin but she wasn't; some say they married secretly and loved one another deeply and mysteriously until their deaths. We know they lie here side by side, almost in each other's arms, and who knows, perhaps their spirits are still together in this cathedral holding hands and binding hearts together.'

'Oh, that's very sad and lovely,' Catherine said.

'He was a truly great man and well loved by the people of Dublin. He was generous to the poor and helpful to the unfortunate and he never turned away anybody genuinely in want. You should know there was another young lady who loved him very greatly. Her name was Vanessa and it's said that she died of a broken heart because he had eyes only for his beloved Stella.'

'But was he not very cranky?' Patsy asked.

'Cranky? He was extremely angry at all kinds of unfairness and poverty and oppression but that didn't stop him living and caring for people. Yes, he was cranky but with cause, and remained so until his death. Do you see what is written on his gravestone? "...*ubi saeva indignatio ulterius cor lacerare nequit*", which means "...where fierce anger can no more wrench at his heart". Dean Swift only found peace from his great indignation at the ills and greed of the world when he went to this burial place next to his Stella.'

Chapter 16

What a great old fella the verger was. Should have asked his name and all. Reminded me of Barry Fitzgerald as the priest in Going My Way. *And the way he told the story of Jonathan Swift and Stella. You could see from looking at the faces of Gurky, Catherine and Eileen that he was making a grand job of it. Lovely voice, deep and laughing but also sad.*

His words seemed to just stay in the air for a while after he'd stopped speaking. I must go back sometime on my own, or maybe with Catherine. See if I can meet him again. What do I call him? Verger? Sir? He said he wasn't a "Father". What do the people call their priests in the Church of Ireland? I don't know. I'll have to find out.

We had a smashing day. After we left St Patrick's, we wandered up to Christchurch Place and passed the tenements where me grandfather was born. Patrick Fagan: I was called after him. His father was called Austen; queer name that. I never knew him as he died before I was born. We were all in a good mood after listening to the old verger and I wanted to show Gurky and the girls the old doss house that used to stand in Back Lane but I couldn't find the building.

Da told me all about it and that it was still going when he was a little boy. The dossers, that's the down-and-outs, used to go there for a bed but there was only a small handful of beds. It was called the "Standing Up Doss House" cause only a few men could lie down and the rest had to stand and wait for a bed to become free. They could be waiting all night and still not get a bed, so there were leather straps fixed to all the walls that the men could put around their chest, under their arms, which could be tightened around their back, and they just flopped forward to let the strap take the weight of their bodies.

Da said the strap often cut into their armpits but they were so tired and weak, they hardly noticed. Can you imagine that? Like a huge cloakroom in a school with rack after rack of coat hangers but instead of kids hanging up coats, men were hung up to rest. Must've been awful to see. All the poor aul fellas hanging there, their legs giving out from under them and they just slung there, more than a hundred of them, trying to sleep.

If you were lucky and made a good impression in the doss house, one of the superintendents might lend you five shillings to go and hire a barrel organ in Golden Lane for a day. You could wheel it all over Dublin playing it and get what money you could, and pay back the five bob, and still have enough for a bed in a proper doss house without having to go back and hang up in the Standing Up Doss House for another session.

I wonder what they did with the women? Do you have dosser women? You couldn't surely hang them up like that, especially if one of them was having a baby. I bet Jonathan Swift wouldn't have allowed a Standing Up Doss House when he was alive. Sometimes you wonder if we're going backwards or forwards in the world. Granny used to take Da and Aunt Peggy, when they were small, to the Daisy Market just behind that doss house to get them second-hand clothes. Socks were a penny a pair.

Poor aul granny put grandad's black suit into the pawn shop at Leonard's Corner every Monday morning—pledging your clothes it was called—and got it out again on a Saturday night to put it on him to go to Mass on a Sunday morning. Off came the suit after Mass and was brushed down ready for the pawn again on Monday morning. Gas the way they lived.

Ma told me that she and Da had to do a bit of pawning themselves when they first got married; she said he was really upset when he had to pawn the gramophone in the pawnshop in Fleet St. "What could we do? We were broke and nobody else had money to lend." You'd imagine they hated it, living like that but I've heard granny and Da say they wouldn't change anything for all the tea in China.

Still, I don't think we've got anything like a Standing Up Doss House in Dublin now. I hope not anyway. Da would know, or the old verger. I could ask him the next time I see him. He's very old. I hope he doesn't die. He's got a young face though, especially when he smiles, and his teeth looked as if they were his own. He wasn't moving them around the way old people do when they've false teeth, like Great Aunt Lizzie. You can see her shifting her false teeth around in her mouth.

Sometimes she forgets to keep her mouth shut when she's doing it and a bit slips out through her lips and then she has to put her hand up to her mouth to *shove it back in again. I hate it when they move their teeth around. You can see them licking the back of the plate. I suppose they need to clean them and get bits of food off that gets trapped or stuck. I'm really glad the verger had his own teeth.*

'Stella and Jonathan are buried together,' said Catherine. 'I wonder where Vanessa is lying.'

'Which one was Vanessa?' Gurky asked.

'The old man said she loved Swift but he loved Stella and she broke her heart over him,' answered Eileen.

'I remember reading somewhere,' said Catherine, 'that Vanessa was very jealous of Stella and she wrote to Stella telling her how much she loved Swift. She was hoping Stella would give up Swift and let her have a chance with him. Somehow Swift heard about the letter and what Vanessa had written and he was mad with anger, and he went to see Vanessa and had an awful row with her.'

'After that, she became destitute and wouldn't even look after her child. They took the child away from her and she became ill and died. I wish I knew where she was buried.'

'I didn't know you knew so much about Jonathan Swift,' said a clearly surprised Patsy.

'You're not the only one who reads anything, Master Patsy Fagan, or who's interested in our history and all the famous people who've lived here.'

'But it was the first time you'd ever visited the cathedral,' answered Patsy, with more than a hint of triumphalism.

'Yes, it was and I thank you for that, dear guide. Maybe you'll take up guiding people around Dublin when you leave school,' teased Catherine.

'Maybe I will.'

'Didn't you know, Catherine, that Patsy owned Dublin and every bit of its history?' Eileen said.

'I wish to Jaysus yis would stop rabbiting on about feckin history and talk instead about sensible things like what picture are we going to see today and where we're buying the fish and chips your Da is treating us to,' said Gurky.

'Have you got a picture in mind?' Eileen asked.

'I thought maybe *Loving You* with Elvis,' answered Gurky with a slight swivel of the hips and a perceptible curling of the upper lip. 'Or else *Shane*, which I hear is really great. It's got Alan Ladd in it.'

'Please, not Elvis, and anyway I hear it's a lousy picture with no story or anything,' pleaded Eileen.

'Ok,' said Gurky quickly, wanting to please Eileen. 'We'll forget Elvis and go to *Shane*.'

'That's very decent of you, Gurky,' said Catherine. 'I suppose you've given serious consideration to *Tammy* and *Carousel*, which are both showing in town.'

'Paul Anka is in some picture but I don't know the name of it,' said Eileen, 'but he sings "Diana" in it.'

'Oh Jesus, Mary and Joseph,' groaned Gurky. 'Not Paul Anka. He has to wear stilts in every film he's so short.'

'I think the best thing is to write all the suggestions on bits of paper and put them in a bag and pick one and we all stick to whatever comes out,' said Patsy.

'Good idea,' Catherine said.

'But,' said Eileen, staring hard at Gurky. 'No Elvis Presley. I'm afraid he'd put me off dancing for at least a fortnight.'

'That's OK with me,' replied Gurky. 'Though I still think he's the greatest and the king of Rock and Roll. I'll just have to go see it with Reddy.'

'Where'll we get a pencil and paper?' Catherine asked.

'We can go into Christ Church Cathedral,' said Patsy. 'There's bound to be something at the back of the church to write with.'

'Go into another feckin church,' said Gurky nearly choking. 'They'll make shaggin saints out of us, I'm telling yis! Three churches in one day, even if two of them are Protestant. Do they have Protestant saints?'

'I've never been in here before either,' said Catherine, 'so I'd like a look around and there's hours to go yet before the pictures.'

'We could see if we can find a pub and have a jar, but I've got an awful shaggin feeling we're going to hear about some aul feckin fella that's buried up to his neck in concrete or worse,' answered Gurky.

'Right you are, Gurky,' said Patsy enthusiastically. 'In here is one of the most famous tombs in the whole of Ireland. C'mon, I'll show you.'

'Oh, Jesus, Mary and Joseph, help us for God Almighty's sake,' intoned a suffering Gurky.

They followed Patsy to a marble tomb with the effigies of a medieval knight in full armour and a child, lying side by side.

'The tomb of Strongbow and his son,' said Patsy.

'Who was he?' Eileen whispered.

'His real name was Richard de Clare,' Patsy answered. 'He was the Earl of Pembroke. But everybody knew him as Strongbow. He led an army of Normans sent by Henry II to capture Dublin from the Danes in 1170.'

'Was he in love with anybody?' Eileen asked.

'He had a wife when he came here,' answered Patsy, 'so I suppose he was in love with her. Her name was Eva and her uncle was Laurence O' Toole who became the patron saint of Dublin. When Strongbow took the city, Henry II came and visited and received Holy Communion here on Christmas Day 1171. Henry called a new street that was being made just up the road a bit "Thomas Street" after Thomas Becket, a bishop that had been murdered in a cathedral in England.

'Everybody said that the King Henry II was responsible for his death, so he went around everywhere for years naming places after this Thomas so that he might be forgiven for having him killed, and get a few years cut off his sentence in Purgatory.'

'They must've been awful shaggin savage to kill a bishop in a cathedral,' said Gurky, finding himself drawn into the story despite his hostility to any further history on this day.

'Shush, Gurky, watch your language! You're in a church,' said Catherine sternly.

'I suppose they were Protestants who killed him?' Gurky asked.

'No,' answered Patsy. 'There were no Protestants. It was about three hundred and fifty years before the first Protestants came with the Reformation. They were all Catholics, Henry II, Strongbow, Laurence O' Toole and Thomas Becket. Do yous want to see the casket where they keep Laurence O'Toole's heart?'

'Oh Jesus, I feel sick again,' said Eileen. 'We've had all the burning of bodies and dogs without heads, and now it's hearts in boxes. It's disgusting, I'm telling yous!'

They found paper and pencil and sat in a pew at the back of the cathedral to write the names of their chosen films. The cathedral organ began to play and was joined by a choir in practice. Patsy, sat next to Catherine, was paralysed with the beauty of the singing and music. He felt unable to move and listened intently to Mozart's Ave Verum Corpus.

He felt Catherine take his hand and squeeze it gently and knew she was feeling the music as he was. He had heard great music many times in churches but this was the first time he had heard this and his heart was dancing to the sounds. He heard Catherine mouthing the Latin words into his ear as she joined in softly with the practice:

Ave verum corpus—Hail, true body
Natum de Maria Virgine—born of the Virgin Mary, Vere passum, immolatum—verily suffered, sacrificed
In cruce pro homine—upon the Cross for mankind.
Cujus latus perforatum—From whose pierced side
Unda fluxit et sanguine—flow water and blood; Esto nobis praegustatum— that we may have a foretaste
In mortis examine—Of our death.

The sweetness of the melody and mystery of the words went to the depths of his soul and lifted him to the heights of ecstasy as he began a love affair with such music as this that he knew would last forever. As Catherine translated line by line, he knew what was meant by mystical power.

The chosen film was *Shane* and, much to the surprise of the girls, all four enjoyed it enormously. There was the evidence of tears in Eileen's and Catherine's eyes when the lights of the cinema were turned on, brought about, they admitted later, by the final scene which shows a young boy shouting his love to the hero, Shane, as he rides off into the sunset never to return, having saved the good and destroyed the bad.

The girls were saved from Gurky's questions as the audience stood silently to attention for the National Anthem. As they left the Savoy Cinema in O'Connell St and headed south, Gurky could hardly restrain himself so excited was he by the film.

'It must've been great to be the fastest draw,' he said. 'Did yis see when Alan Ladd went for his gun in the saloon and Jack Palance was standing there with that evil grin on his face?'

'Course we did, we were there,' answered Patsy. 'And it was Jack Palance who went for his gun first, not Alan Ladd.'

'Yeah, and Jack Palance thought he was great, wearing two guns and all. He was OK when he was shooting at poor aul farmers and that class of thing but when he met his match, he was no good at all even though the hero was only wearing one gun. If you was living in the Wild West, Patsy, how many guns would you wear?'

'I don't know. Probably only one, like Alan Ladd.'

'Me too, if one is good enough for Alan Ladd then it's good enough for me.'

'Are yous two cowboys hungry, cause I'm starving,' said Eileen. 'Where are we going to get our fish and chips?'

'If we walk back up to Lord Edward St, near Christchurch Hill, we can have the best fish and chips in Dublin,' said Patsy.

'That's a long way,' answered Eileen. 'Is there no where nearer?'

'There's lots of places nearer but Burdock's is the very best chipper in the city, I'm telling yous. And it won't take long if we step it out smartly, and then we can eat them walking back down Dame St and catch the bus home in South Great George's St.'

'I'm game for the best fish and chips in Dublin,' said Catherine. 'And the walk'll certainly put an edge on my appetite.'

'I don't need a shaggin edge,' said Gurky. 'C'mon, let's go before I drop dead this minute with the feckin starvation.'

Along O'Connell St they strode, the last rays of the June sun still catching the windows of the top floor of Clery's department store. They turned right into Bachelor's Walk and carried on until they reached the Halfpenny Bridge and crossed the Liffey, short cutting their way through the deserted narrow streets and lanes of the Temple Bar area until they emerged out again into the busy Parliament St, leading to City Hall.

'Nearly there,' cried Patsy. 'I'll race yous to the shop, c'mon!'

'Wait for me, you bugger,' shouted Gurky, and set off after him.

'You're terribly out of breath,' said Mr Burdock, the owner of the shop. 'You must be in bad condition and yous only young ones. Are you sure fish and chips will be good for yous?'

'We've run all the way from the Savoy Cinema in O'Connell St,' Gurky fibbed.

'Not all the way but a bit of it,' Catherine corrected.

'Well, yous must be very hungry after a marathon like that. Right, what'll it be?'

'Cod for me,' said Eileen.

'And me,' added Catherine.

'I'll have ray,' said Patsy.

'And I'll have the biggest shaggin piece of haddock ever taken out of the ocean,' said Gurky, practising his fastest draw with his right hand, shaped into the barrel and gun butt of a Wild West six-shooter.

I think that's when I loved Catherine most. Always making the best of things, trying to keep people together, finding how to make peace. She had that gift, yet she was very determined and could cut the skin off you with her tongue if she needed to. She never let Reddy or Gurky, or me for that matter, get away with bad language. Her voice was lovely when she sang the "Ave Verum Corpus" in my ear and told me what the words meant.

"Where did you learn that?" I asked her.

"In the school choir."

"But you sang it so well and knowing all the Latin and what it meant."

"Thank you, kind sir. Perhaps when we go to Sandymount we'll both sing in the school choir."

I was mad to find out for her where Jonathan Swift's Vanessa was buried so I slipped out of Da's garage and went around the corner to some second-hand bookshops near Lincoln Place. There were plenty of books by Swift and about Swift and lots of stuff about his relationships with Stella and Vanessa, but I couldn't find any mention about where she was buried. I was nearly ready to give up when a nice looking fella of about 25 came over to me and asked if he could help.

He spoke with a really posh accent and he was wearing steel-rim glasses like the ones James Joyce wore in a photograph they put in all the books about him. I told the fella I was trying to find where Vanessa was buried and he seemed a bit surprised and amused, and he said it was a very unusual question. In fact, no one had ever asked him before and he was a bit embarrassed because he didn't know the answer, and he said he was all the more embarrassed because he had studied English literature at Trinity College, Dublin, and he should know.

I liked him cause he was so honest and he didn't try to worm his way out of it and he was really interested in why I was so set on finding Vanessa's grave. I told him about our visit to St Patrick's and about Swift and Stella and the old verger. I said I'd thought I'd go back and ask the verger as I was sure he'd know the answer, but as Lincoln Place and Clare St with the book shops were so close to Da's garage in Westland Row, it was easier for me to go there but if I couldn't find out, then I'd go back to St Patrick's.

I was really pleased when the fella, he told me his name was Rory and he was training to be an "antiquarian", said I could come back a couple of days later if I was back in the garage and he'd find out for me. I thought that was really great and I was as pleased as punch. And sure enough, when I went back, he gave me a really warm welcome, as if we'd been friends all our lives, and he called me Patsy and told me to call him Rory.

"Your friend Catherine is sure to be disappointed I'm afraid, Patsy. Vanessa is not buried in a cathedral or even a church graveyard. The best account I can find is that she was buried in what was once burial ground for the ancient church of St Andrew that stood originally in Palace St near Dublin Castle. However, the old church has now disappeared and much of the area was levelled and cleared during the 19th century and the present church of St Andrew was completed in 1866.

"Looking at the old records, the nearest estimate we can make for the exact location of Vanessa's grave is under the roadway beside McCullough Pigott's in Suffolk St."

We didn't get to the dance in the De La Salle school after all the plans for Gurky to go with Eileen. She was looking forward to it really and I'd say she was actually hoping that Gurky might try to hold her hand. She wasn't up to any kissing or that class of thing and she let him know it. After all, she wasn't old enough, just gone 13, a year younger than myself but as me Ma said, a year at that age can make a big difference.

I was OK for a bit of kissing and so was Catherine, though she wouldn't hold a kiss for as long as I wanted to, and when I did manage to go on for a bit longer than usual, she'd come up for air all breathing and steaming like she was going to burst a head gasket, and her creamy skin turning red and almost purple. Anyway, the reason we didn't go to the dance was because Gurky was messing about with some fellas from school trying to make a really strong banger like the firework ones you can buy in England but that are banned in Ireland.

They had a piece of lead pipe and had beaten one end of it closed with a hammer. They took it to the Glen where we played cowboys and Indians when we were younger, and started to fill the hollow pipe with different stuff. Gurky told me later they put in saltpetre, sulphur, some charcoal and weed killer. It was another fella who had already left school who brought the stuff. He was older than us and came from Dundrum, and he had told some of the kids living in our area that if they wanted to see a real banger and not just a toy job, they should go to the landfill dump in the Glen.

Gurky was holding the pipe on a concrete block, trying not to spill any of the ingredients from it, and the fella from Dundrum started to beat the open end to close it. The idea, as the police explained later, was to throw the sealed pipe on a bonfire and when the pipe was hot enough, it would explode. The police said it could easily have killed somebody if it had been exploded like that.

As it was, the hammering must have caused a spark because the pipe blew up in Gurky's hand and blew the first finger of his right hand off, and took away half his thumb as well. The ambulance took him to the Meath Hospital in Long Lane where he had to stay for nearly two weeks. The kids in Landscape went looking for the finger and bit of thumb that Gurky lost, and a fella in our school brought in a burnt bit of finger with the nail still on it, all black and in tatters. We took it and buried it in Gurky's garden without his Ma or Da knowing anything about it.

Of course, we didn't feel like going to the dance after that and Eileen and Catherine did a lot of crying, and so did Reddy: "I'd love to get me hands on that ballocks from Dundrum who brought that stuff along." In fact, the police had already arrested him but we never heard what happened to him. Me, Eileen, Catherine, and Reddy went to see Gurky in the hospital when he was up and about, and you wouldn't believe it, but he was in a good mood.

"No more writing for me before I leave school, yis know what I mean? And I want to show yis something I've been practising all week." He stood out in front of the four of us and said, "Watch now cause I'm very quick," and he drew his left hand as if he was holding a cowboy's gun from an imaginary holster on his left hip. "There yis are, still the fastest draw in the west."

Chapter 17

Catherine and Eileen completed a novena for Gurky Ryan's recovery. They visited the nearest nine churches to where they lived over a period of nine days and said nine Hail Marys, nine Our Fathers and nine Glory Be's to the Father, Son and Holy Ghost as offerings for Gurky; they also lit a candle in each of the nine churches on his behalf.

While Gurky's friends and family were storming the gates of Heaven with their prayers, other misfortunes and accidents happened in the Landscape area. Reddy Costello was climbing high in a chestnut tree when he fell to ground from a height of about twenty feet. His fall was cushioned considerably by the numerous branches he smashed through in his descent and he missed impaling himself on the spiked iron railing over which he had trespassed to get to the chestnut tree by no more than eighteen inches.

Bruised, swollen, crying, and feeling thoroughly miserable but otherwise undamaged, he limped home with the help of Patsy and Dinny Fagan. Two days later, Dinny climbed onto the back of a pickup-truck, parked outside the Fagans' home, which his father was delivering to a customer. Tom Fagan did not spot his son in the back of the truck as he got into the driver's seat and started the engine. He drove off with the hapless Dinny trying to conceal himself in the back.

Dinny panicked when he realised he had no idea where his father was going or when he might next stop, so he jumped off the back when the truck was travelling, "not all that fast I think". He collided with a wooden telegraph pole and ended up unconscious in the Meath Hospital not far from where Gurky lay. Fortunately, he suffered no more than severe concussion, cuts and bruising, but he too had a period of time in hospital recovering. Catherine and Eileen added him to the names of Gurky and Reddy when interceding with God and the Blessed Virgin.

A week after Dinny's escapade, Patsy Fagan was crossing the Churchtown Rd and stopped halfway to allow an oncoming Morris Minor to pass. As the motor car drew level with him, the driver's door flew open and struck Patsy full on the side of his body knocking him several feet back across the way he had come. The sounds of the "thud" from the car door hitting human flesh and bone, and the screech of skidding tyres as the driver stood on his brakes, brought a number of shoppers rushing out of Miss Cooney's grocery shop.

They saw a crumpled Patsy by the side of the road and the driver of the Morris Minor drag himself from his car only for his legs to buckle under him, so badly shaken was he. He simply sat with his back against the rear wheel of his car looking across to where Patsy was lying and turned first pale and then green before getting sick in the road. The shoppers had gathered around our young hero and a calm Miss Cooney had come out of her shop with a basin full of water and a cloth to minister to the wounded boy.

Even before it was thought necessary to send for an ambulance, Patsy was sat up asking Miss Cooney to go easy with the water and there was no need to drown him.

'Are you able to get up, Patsy?' she asked, 'or shall we send for your Ma and da?'

'I'm alright, Miss Cooney,' answered Patsy. 'I'm just a bit winded, that's all. What's wrong with your man, over there? Did he get hit as well?'

'No. That's the driver of the car that hit you. He's feeling very bad and sick with the shock of it, that's all.'

Someone had gone to Patsy's home and Tom Fagan sprinted the hundred yards to get to see what had befallen his son. He pushed through the small group of people and saw Patsy sitting up, drinking a glass of water that Miss Cooney had handed him. Patsy smiled at his father.

'I'm alright, Da, the door just bounced off me and I was winded.'

'Jaysus Christ Almighty,' exclaimed Tom Fagan, almost as a prayer, 'is somebody to be killed before this madness stops? First Gurky, then that eegit Reddy, your brother, Dinny, and now you. Yous will put your mother and me in the feckin madhouse.'

'It wasn't his fault at all, Mr Fagan,' said Miss Cooney. 'There's the driver of the car sitting over there. He's already explained that the door of his car flew open as he was driving along, and poor Patsy was standing in the middle of the road waiting for him to go by before crossing and got a belt of a Morris Minor door for his troubles.'

'What's the matter with him?' Tom Fagan asked.

'He's just feeling very shocked and sick that's all,' Miss Cooney answered.

'I should think so too,' said Tom Fagan. 'If he's driving around in cars with their doors flying open, he has a right to be feeling sick. Has anyone called the police?'

'No, as soon as I knew Patsy wasn't seriously hurt, I didn't consider it necessary meself to call the police,' replied Miss Cooney. 'The poor man's had an awful fright and he'd find it cruel now to have to answer a lot of questions from some big Guarda. I'm sure he didn't want the door to fly open.'

Tom Fagan did not want to appear unreasonable in front of his neighbours in Landscape and Patsy seemed none the worse for his adventure. Nonetheless, he walked to the Morris Minor and examined the offending door and its locking mechanism. He slammed the door closed a number of times and tried without success to open the door without depressing the metal tongue which prevents the door from opening freely.

'Seems OK,' he said to no one in particular.

'I think it wasn't closed properly when I stopped with my wife yesterday after we did some shopping. I'm terribly sorry and I can't tell you how relieved I am that the lad isn't badly hurt.'

'Well, luckily, he's OK, though I suspect he'll have some bruising tomorrow. You look badly shaken yourself. Do you want to come home with us and the missis will make you a cup of tea?'

'That's very decent of you, and yes please, because I don't think I'll be able to drive the car for a while yet.'

'Ok, well, leave it where it is and you can pick it up later on if you feel up to it.'

'Thanks very much. That's grand, and the funny thing is, I've been thinking of changing that car for something bigger, you know, something better built, you know, with more space and everything.'

'Is that so? Come on, Patsy, I'll give you a hand. There y'are, that's it, we'll manage. What's your name?' Tom Fagan asked the driver.

'Matt O'Reilly.'

'Well, come on and meet the wife, Matt. And tell me more now about the sort of car you have in mind.'

The last days of the long summer term in school were quickly approaching and Patsy Fagan was already busy preparing for September and his new school in Sandymount. He had visited the second-hand bookshops around Clare St with his mother to buy school textbooks and he introduced her to Rory, whom he now considered to be his friend. For his part, Rory took Patsy's list of required texts and managed to find second-hand copies, all in excellent condition.

Next, Patsy had to be kitted out with school uniform. He had never worn school uniform in the past as neither Marymount nor Milltown schools had uniforms. The school outfitters off Grafton St were not remotely cheap and Patsy felt pangs of guilt as his mother dug deeply for scarce pound notes. He had overheard a conversation taking place between his parents that caused him a deal of anxiety. Tom Fagan had been deliberately casual in his opening remarks to his wife, but Patsy fancied he felt strongly his father's doubts.

'I hope, Nuala, we can go on as we are for a long time yet.'

'What do you mean, Tom?'

'Well, we're hanging on, you know, just about, but I'm hoping of course that things will get better, sooner rather than later.'

'How bad is it then?' Nuala asked.

'If things stay the same for too much longer, I think we'd have to consider a move to England. You know what I'm saying, don't you?'

'Sell the house and everything and move to England?'

'Yes, but there's loads of work there, just for the asking. Tony keeps saying in his letters there's stacks of work and I'd have me choice in Coventry.'

'Coventry doesn't sound all that nice from what Tony says,' Nuala answered, tears coming to her eyes.

'It wouldn't have to be Coventry. Your man, Matt O'Reilly that I sold the Dodge to, has just come back from England, rolling in money. He was in a place in Kent not too far from London and he said there are great opportunities for anyone who's not afraid of a bit of hard work.'

'It'd be a great pity, Tom, if we had to go. What with Patsy starting in the high school and Eileen and Dinny getting on so well in their schools. And now with another baby coming next February, please God...'

'Been able to pay the bills and knowing where the food is coming from is more important than schooling, Nuala,' he answered, somewhat vexed.

'I know, Tom,' she said, trying to soften him. 'Anyway, you said we can hang on for some time even if things don't get better. How long?'

'How long what?'

'How long can we hang on, stay here, before we'd have to go?'

'I hope everything gets better and we won't have to go. The government is making a right kip of the country and people just haven't got the money to spend on cars or anything else for that shaggin matter.'

'How long, Tom?'

'About a year. But pray that business will pick up.'

Patsy had chilled to the bone when he heard his parents' words and determined he would cost them as little as possible as far as his new school was concerned. Rory had got him bargains with the books and he would ride to school no matter what the weather, rather than cost bus fares. Furthermore, he would go to his father's garage to help out as often as possible during weekdays and also on Saturdays, and he would work hard with Nasty to make the cars look attractive to potential customers. And he would pray his father's fortunes would improve.

I know Tony says it's good over there but I want to stay here. I want to finish school and I want to play rugby and go to Landsdowne Rd. I still have a lot of finding out about Dublin and all...

He felt shame at the surge of selfishness and blushed at the meanness of his thoughts.

And she's going to have another baby! And what about Gurky and Reddy? Moving to England would mean never seeing them again. And Catherine? Jesus, she was delighted when I told her I'd found out where Vanessa was buried. Rory was right though: she was disappointed the grave had been covered with a tarmac road. Still, we went down there together on a Saturday morning and traffic was everywhere, coming down Grafton St and turning into Suffolk St.

Buses every two seconds and trucks, bikes and taxis, and me still sore from the belt of the Morris Minor door. She'd brought a small posy of flowers from her garden, wrapped in tissue paper, but the nearest we could get to the middle of the road was the edge of the footpath.

"I'm not going to put them in the gutter. What'll I do?"

"Why not put them inside the railings of St Andrew's Churchyard—look just up there, opposite O'Neill's pub?"

"It's too far away. Look, Patsy, I'll put them here."

She'd found a drainpipe on the McCullough-Piggot shop front that had a sort of ornamental cast-iron hopper at its foot. She found a space between the wall and the metal hopper. It started to rain and within seconds, it was lashing and we were both soaked. "Do you think they'll be alright there?" she asked me.

"Of course, c'mon or we'll drown." I noticed she had written a small card and placed it among the flowers. I bent down to look and saw the ink beginning to run with all the rain on it, but I was able to read what she had written before it disappeared:

'Sleep well, Dearest Vanessa. Love, Catherine and Patsy.'

"That's grand. The flowers'll be fine," I said. She lowered her head and whispered a few words, and then we left.

Chapter 18

'So, boys,' announced Mr Bambrick, 'this is our last questions class before you leave us and inflict yourselves on an unsuspecting world. What joy you'll bring to unfortunate managers and foremen and shop owners who think they've had it bad up to now, but wait till they see you Gurky Explosives, and you, Reddy Suicide. And Master Fagan, will you last until you get to your new school or will you play the toreador with Dublin's traffic?'

'What do you mean a "corridor", Sir? I don't understand that one,' said Gurky, his right hand still heavily bandaged and resting in a sling.

'Shut up, Ryan, we haven't started yet. Right to business: I hope we're going to get some excellent questions and even better answers. You're all growing up, even you, Ryan, thank God, though I have my doubts about one or two of you. Do you hear me, Master Costello, and you, Noel Browne?'

'Yes, Sir,' answered Reddy.

'Yes, Sir,' said Noel Browne. 'Me Ma said…'

'Yes, thank you, Browne, no doubt we'll hear what the redoubtable Mrs Browne said later on.'

'Who's going to win the soccer world cup, Sir?' Reddy Costello asked.

'I'm not a fortune-teller, Costello. That wasn't exactly the sort of question I had in mind. Yes, Fagan, what's the question?'

'Why do women have so many babies in Ireland?'

'I'm sorry, Fagan, I don't think I understand the question properly. Can you tell me what you mean?'

There was not a sound in the classroom. Every boy had heard the question and knew somehow that a barrier had been breached. Reddy Costello had urged his friend to ask the question but had not been prepared for it to be actually asked. Mr Bambrick was uncertain whether the question stemmed from an innocence born simply of spontaneous curiosity, or if it referred to the question of birth

146

control. He needed more information before he could respond or allow further comments from other pupils.

'I mean, Sir,' answered Patsy, 'that the married women in Ireland, like me ma, and lots of other fellas' mothers, have loads of babies and are always having to go into hospital to have them, or have to feed them and wash them. The mothers have stacks of work to do all the time and they're always carrying babies around in their bellies or in their arms.'

'That's a filthy thing to say,' called out an indignant Noel Browne.

'You'll get your turn, Browne,' the teacher replied, not yet certain what Patsy was implying. 'What would you have them do, Fagan? The mothers, I mean.'

'I'm not sure, Sir, but I hear that in other countries they don't have to have babies if they don't want, and they can make sure they have only the number of babies they do want. It could even be just one or two. Do you know what I mean, Sir?'

'Yes, I think I've got hold of it now, Fagan. But tell me, in what you've heard about other countries have you heard how they manage to have fewer babies than mothers do in Ireland?'

'Yes, Sir,' answered an increasingly worried Patsy, who knew there was no turning back now. 'The men put little balloons on their eh...sorry, Sir, the only respectable name I know for it is, em, their mickey, Sir. And the little balloon stops the man's stuff getting into the woman. And if they do want a baby, they don't have the little balloon.'

Again, there was complete silence for about ten seconds almost as if no one wanted to draw breath.

'This is disgusting,' called out Noel Browne. 'Just wait till I tell my ma...'

'Be quiet, Browne,' Mr Bambrick said firmly. 'And that goes for everybody else; be very still and think for a few moments.'

The teacher had to decide whether to bar all further discussion of the subject of birth control or to allow further views to be expressed or other questions to be asked. He could not be certain that every boy in the class of forty knew even the basic facts of reproduction or had a clear idea of what generally constituted sexual relations between men and women. He was acutely aware that to allow the debate to go on could result in his dismissal from his post with practically no possibility of future employment in Irish schools.

Birth control, or more accurately, artificial birth control was hugely controversial, and the very mention of it was considered in many quarters, not exclusively ecclesiastical, to be wickedly sinful. Contraceptives were officially banned from Ireland and to smuggle them in with the purpose of selling them was a criminal offence. Those people who had contact with family members or friends to-ing and fro-ing from Britain had a regular supply if they wanted them.

Undoubtedly, many Irish women would have refused to have anything to do with contraceptives no matter how many children they had or how short they were of money. They believed with burning ferocity the teachings of the church, and no more strongly than where that teaching touched upon matters of the flesh. Mr Bambrick considered if he could steer a safe way to port yet allow the question to be pursued.

'Do you not like babies, Patsy Fagan?' he asked.

'Of course I do, Sir. I'm not saying…'

'Would you prefer if some of your brothers or sisters had not been born?'

'That's not what I'm saying at all, Sir…'

'Is there anybody in the class who wishes that one of their brothers or sisters had not been born?'

'He's not saying that,' called out Reddy Costello, feeling angry and hot.

'Oh, and what is he saying, Costello?'

'He's saying that our mas are worn out with all the babies they have and why can't they have a rest from babies for a while if a little balloon will help.'

'I'm assuming that all boys in this, the senior class in the school, know the basic biological facts of human reproduction. If you don't, you should at your age, and if any of you do not know about the birds and bees, then I suggest you ask your friends or older brothers or take your father aside and ask him.

'If he laughs and says babies are found under cabbages, or any other vegetable for that matter, laugh back at him and say: "Listen, Da, I'm leaving school this month and I know that babies don't come from under cabbages because I went out into the garden last night and I didn't find a single one. Now come on, give me the awful truth. I'll take it like a man. I'll make you proud of me, Da!".'

It took a long time for the laughter to die down in Mr Bambrick's. What tickled his pupils to near hysteria was the thought of asking their fathers to tell them anything about what went on between men and women in the privacy of their bedrooms.

'Ok, now back to the question posed by Masters Fagan and Costello. They have asked, boys, about a subject known as "artificial birth control". Now that means that scientists, often medical doctors, have discovered ways of preventing women from becoming pregnant. By "women", I mean of course "wives". Husbands and wives live together and have a very special relationship with each other.

'I can see from the sniggering that you understand me. Wives become pregnant from this special relationship, not on every occasion, you understand, but often enough. That means they have babies.'

'But they don't have to have one every year or sometimes even two in the same year, do they?' Patsy pleaded.

'Well, husbands and wives can decide not to have that special relationship that often ends up in a pregnancy, you know.'

Enough of the more mature members of the class found themselves sneering at this suggestion, and Mr Bambrick was soon regretting his decision to carry on with the topic.

'That's not realistic, Sir.'

'I can't imagine my old man taking kindly to your advice, Sir.'

'My aul fella would say he's not a shaggin priest with all the fasting and absence they sign up to, taking their vows of poverty and celibacy and all.'

'"Abstinence and "celibacy",'" corrected Mr Bambrick, never missing an opportunity to teach.

'Whatever, Sir. I don't understand what's wrong with the thing, what's its name, you know, the proper name for the balloons.'

'They're called contraceptives, Master Doyle,' answered Mr Bambrick, relieved that the pupil had brought the conversation back to where he felt it was on safer ground. 'What's wrong with them is the fact that Holy Mother Church has declared their use to be grievously sinful.'

'Yeah,' shouted Reddy Costello, but why are they sinful? They're not doing anybody any harm, are they? And you could even say they'd be doing a lot of our mas a power of good.'

'They're sinful because the church says that to interfere with the natural process of the, em, what did I call it, ah yes, the special relationship between husbands and wives is sinful. The church teaches that the purpose of marriage is so that children may be born. But the church also teaches that husbands and wives, husbands especially, must be responsible and married people should not have children they can't afford to look after.'

'Our Lord never said anything about that though, did He?' Patsy asked.

'Well, they weren't invented in His time, were they?' Reddy asked.

'What weren't invented?' the teacher asked.

'The contraceptives,' answered Reddy. 'They didn't have science or anything like that when Our Lord was around. So how could He have said something was sinful if He didn't even know about it?'

'Do remember who you're talking about, Master Costello, and be very respectful. May I remind you that Jesus, as one of the Divine Trinity, knows everything there is to know, past, present and future. No secret or thought can escape Him. And I suspect you might be surprised at the amount of "science", as you put it, people in ancient times did know.'

'But,' persisted Reddy, 'he wasn't going around when He was doing the miracles, getting cripples to walk and the poor aul blind fellas to see and all, thinking in His head about the em... what do you call them, the contradictive, was He? Otherwise, it's common sense he would've said something about it.'

'Sir?' Noel Browne persisted, who had been trying desperately hard to draw the schoolteacher's attention for the last ten minutes.

'Yes, Browne?'

'You should thrash Costello within an inch of his life for the disgusting and disgraceful things he's been saying about Our Blessed Lord. That's what my Ma would do.'

'Why don't you come and try and do it yourself, you dopey ballocks. I know what I'd like to do to you and your ma.'

'Costello!' Mr Bambrick shouted, feeling a great deal of sympathy for Reddy. 'Remember what happened last time you lost control of yourself? No more bad language. Now try to remember, Our Lord gave authority to His followers to decide what were sins and what weren't.'

'But, Sir,' called Patsy, 'I'm one of His followers and I can't see how it's a sin. You're saving all those mothers loads of work and all, and it's not as if you're doing anybody any harm.'

'Well, you're hardly a Doctor or Father of the church now, are you? You are not yet what we might call Learned.'

'Ok, Sir,' conceded Patsy, 'but you said that the artificial birth control, right, was interfering with nature or, I think you said, the natural process.'

'That's right.'

'But we've just had our inoculations to stop us getting diphtheria and other diseases. So, we're interfering with the natural process because we should try to fight the disease without using medicine.'

'It's a good argument, Fagan, but as I said, the learned Doctors and Fathers of the Church, and also the Holy Father himself, have the authority of Our Lord to decide what is sinful and what is not.'

'But he's not a daddy, is he?' Gurky Ryan shouted out.

'Who exactly is not a daddy?' Mr Bambrick enquired.

'The Holy Father,' answered Gurky. 'They call him the Holy Father but he's not a daddy. There's no kids calling him "Da". Just like our priests here in Dublin, we call them "Father", but they're not real fathers, are they? Though some of them might be. Do yis know what I mean, hey?'

'Careful, Master Ryan. Remember you have one good hand left; that's all that's needed for the stick.'

The debate went on for the remainder of the lesson and Mr Bambrick believed it had been the right decision to allow it to continue. Noel Browne's mother complained to the headmaster and to the parish priest, but nothing seemed to come of her complaints and the "Questions" class enjoyed great popularity all the time Mr Bambrick remained at Milltown.

Chapter 19

Nuala Fagan's father, Patrick Lawler, was dead. He had been living with his daughter's family since he was 75 and he had celebrated his 82nd birthday two days before he left our world, full of hope that the Good Lord would give him a warm welcome into paradise. He was born in 1876, and for the last twelve years of his life, he had been completely blind.

Unlike his son-in law Tom Fagan whose father had been blinded with terrifying rapidity by gas during the First World War, his blindness had come about gradually, caused no doubt his doctor declared by long hours of reading in very poor light. Paddy Lawler was an avid reader and particularly enjoyed Dickens and Trollope. Unfortunately, too much of his reading was done in his bedroom by the smoky light of his paraffin lamp. Some damage to his left eye had also been inflicted by a bull that had attacked and gored him in a field in County Kildare.

His neighbours and friends said he was fortunate to have escaped with his life. The bull had knocked him to the ground, tried to trample him, and one of its horns had pierced his cheek and its tip had lodged itself in the palate of his mouth. He managed to dislodge the horn and slide his cheek free, and before the beast could gore him again, he took hold of both its horns in his hands, raised his upper body so that his head was positioned above the bull's massive skull, and with every ounce of strength he had left in his body, he bit deeply into the base of one of the bull's ears.

He felt his teeth cutting into the tough hide and tasted the animal's blood in his mouth. There was no movement from the bull, and he and it remained entirely still until two passing farmworkers spotted him and the animal and came to the rescue. When he recovered from his ordeal, he said that seeing through his left eye was like looking through a dirty window.

His wife had given birth to four girls: Biddy, the eldest, born delicate, and destined to live her life in a sanatorium run by the Sisters of Mercy until she died in her 40s; then came Nuala, sparkling, bright, pretty, full of life and game for any adventure; next arrived Mollie with the same eagerness for life and love as her older sister; last was Susan who went to live in London while still in her teens, and died a young woman, of tuberculosis.

Their mother, Mary, had died only days after Susan's birth when Nuala was 6 years old. Their father, unable to care for four young girls on his own, looked to his relatives to take them in and bring them up as their own, but he never stopped loving them, and travelled long distances on his old upright bicycle to different parts of the county and to Dublin to visit each one.

He had made his living during the first years of his marriage working on farms, cutting turf and odd jobbing here and there. In the 1930s, when three of his girls were settled and living with their aunts, and Biddy was in a convent home, he set off to find work in the shipyards on the Clyde. He scrimped and saved, going regularly to bed early, so as not to spend too much time in pubs with cronies spending all he earned.

He returned to working on farms in Co Kildare in 1938, and with the money he had saved in Glasgow, bought half a dozen small fields, scattered around the area of Kildangan, which he let to local farmers for grazing.

Soon after Nuala married Tom Fagan, her father was a frequent visitor to Harold's Cross and to Landscape when the family moved there. He loved his grandchildren and had a special soft spot for Dinny and Mollie. Everyone said he became a great expert in sitting in an armchair, rocking a baby gently in his arms, and they marvelled at how even the most cantankerous infant would immediately stop wailing when placed on his lap.

Of his grandchildren, he had seen Tony, Patsy and Eileen as babies but had never seen, Alana, Dinny, Mollie nor of course the new baby, Rosie; yet he could tell each one distinctly, simply from touching their faces with his finger. When he came to live in his daughter's home in Landscape, he knew it was to see out his days. He enjoyed sitting in the garden when the weather was warm and sunny listening to the radio.

He had never learnt to read Braille and so was no longer able to enjoy books. Nor was he the sort of blind man who could find his way around the house by "touch" or memory, despite being able to tell his grandchildren apart through the mere tracing of a finger across a face. He had to be guided and steered when he needed to go from bedroom to toilet, or from upstairs to downstairs, or out into the garden. His rich baritone voice could be heard calling: 'Dinny... Dinny... Dinny,' or 'Patsy...Patsy, come and take me to the john.'

When their parents were not there to box their ears, his grandchildren enjoyed playing jokes on him. Dinny was especially fond of leading him into a linen closet, pretending it was the lavatory, saying cheerfully as he closed the door on his unfortunate grandfather:

'All right, Pop, can you find the pot yourself?'

'Yis, yis, yis,' the old man would reply. 'Thank you, Dinny, thank you. Is there a bit of paper here, will you see?'

'Yeah, just beside the pot, usual place.'

Dinny would close the door with a bang but remained inside the walk-in cupboard to enjoy the spectacle of his grandfather pulling down his long johns, and then bending forward with the palm of his right hand trying to touch the top of the lavatory pot. He would turn left and right, patting the air, and feeling nothing would edge forward a little, repeat the process until at last he would bump into the linen shelves and realise his grandson was playing tricks on him.

'Dinny, you shaggin little gurrier, where are you? I'm in the cupboard. Come back in here, you little blackguard, before I destroy the floor with me number two. You can wait till I see your mam and then you'll get it me boyo.'

He never told Nuala and never anticipated that the same whole process would happen again a week or two later.

They had all the black vestments for the requiem Mass and the dark brown candles on the altar. The smell of the incense gets into your nose and mouth. You can still smell it the next day on your clothes and in your hair. I could smell it in Dinny's hair when we were in bed after the funeral. He fell asleep quickly and I snuggled up to him and I had my nose in his hair and I smelt the incense on him. I was glad he was warm as the smell reminded me of dead people.

I never knew granda had so many relations, whole crowds of them up from the country: "A convention of culchies," Uncle Bill said. "All the aul ones in black, like a murder of crows."

"What's that, a murder of crows?" I asked. He wouldn't tell me.

"The art of scholarship is the ability to find out."

"That's why I'm asking you, I'm trying to find out what it means."

"But finding out must take effort; that's the way you remember. If I tell you the answer, you'll forget it in a week. You must go to some other university and do your work there. I'm closed down for the day, thank you very much."

The Mass for the dead: "They need it to send them on their way," Aunt Maisie explained. "It helps them get through purgatory, so they don't have to stay there too long before joining Jesus in heaven. Old Paddy will soon be with his wife, Mary, you know; she died before yous were born. And he'll be with your little sister, Alana, and all the angels that died when they were just babies, and he'll be rocking Alana on his lap the way he used to, with the pipe in his mouth."

His pipe was like the thurible, throwing big clouds of smoke into the air from the burning incense and charcoal. He had to clean it and empty and fill it by feeling everything with his hands. He sucked and blew and tapped and dampened it and bit the stem with his yellowing teeth. Ma left him an enamel basin so he could empty the pipe into it without spilling bits on the floor and burning the carpet.

He used the basin as an ashtray all the time, feeling for the rim of it with his left hand and running his fingers down the inside till he found the middle of the bottom, and he'd burn himself when there were hot ashes in there. "Oh Mother of God, bring me a cup of cold water," he'd shout, and put the burnt finger in the water to cool and then dip the other fingers and shake and sprinkle the water into the basin of ashes, listening for the sizzle when the water fell on a piece of burning tobacco.

"It'll be your father or Patsy who'll burn us all one day," Da said to Ma. You could see the little burn marks on Mollie's baby's shawl after she'd been in his lap and he'd been smoking the pipe. Ma said he couldn't smoke the pipe any more at the same time as he was holding the baby after Mollie's baby started screaming one day and nearly gave us all a heart attack. Ma ran in and grabbed her from granda's lap. She found a tiny burn mark on her face.

"No more pipe, Daddy, when you're holding the baby. It's too dangerous; you'll set her on fire."

Requiescat in pace, the choir was singing. Rest in peace. Music for the dead. "He loved music, your granda, music and reading," Uncle Bill told me.

"Did he like Mozart?" I asked.

"Ah well, I don't know about that but I'm sure he must have. He was always going into churches listening to organ recitals and all that class of thing, when he could see, you know." I wish I'd asked him myself about Mozart and gone to an organ recital with him. I never asked him about what he liked or didn't like. Too late now, though maybe he'll hear Mozart's music in heaven.

Catherine let me listen to her da's record of Mozart's Requiem Mass. It's the best thing I've ever heard. I mean I like Elvis and Pat Boone and all, and the music we have in our dances in Landscape, there's nothing wrong with it. But I'd have liked the Mozart Requiem sung at granda's Mass. That's what I'd love at my own funeral.

You could imagine floating up high above the altar looking down on your own coffin and all the crowd there, you hope, and the choir singing the Agnus Dei and everybody listening. It'd be marvellous to hear Gurky saying to Reddy, "Wasn't the music shaggin great?"

I think he knew he was going to die that day, mind you. When I brought him up his mug of tea in the morning, he asked me to get the cardboard box from under his bed and put it on his lap. It was the first time he'd ever asked me to get it for him and I'd never seen him open it before. He was sat up with his back against the headboard and he opened the cardboard lid. He lifted out a framed photograph of a lady dressed in old fashion clothes and ran his fingers across the glass and then lifted it to his lips and kissed it softly.

"That's your grandmother," he said. He took out some papers and laid them on the side of the bed. There was a long brown envelope with his name on it and written in large letters "WILL". He found a rosary in the box and kissed the silver crucifix and hung the rosary around his skinny neck. The last item he took out was a battered old book. The paper cover was all brown with tobacco smoke and it looked like it'd been read a million times. He felt the book and opened it and lifted it right up close to his eyes as if he was trying to read it.

"Are you all right, Granda?" I asked him.

"Yis, Yis," he answered, but he was crying a bit and I felt sorry for him and for all the times Dinny and me had played jokes on him.

"What's the matter?" I asked.

"She should have married him, she should have. There was no reason, and she knew she loved him. It was just in her cranky nature that she wouldn't do it. Oh, she made me angry with her silliness. Take the book, Patsy, for yourself. It's the only book I kept after I lost me sight. I couldn't let go of it. It was me favourite story but I did want Lily Dale to marry Johnny Eames." The book was called, The Small House at Allington by Anthony Trollope.

Patrick Lawler was dead and when his fields were auctioned off, each of his daughters received £1500. Nuala Fagan put her arm through her husband's arm as they left the solicitor's office and said: '£1500, Tom, that'll keep us safe for a year or two longer won't it, if we look after it and are careful?'

'It will indeed, me darling, it will indeed.'

There was great excitement in Milltown Boys National School, especially amongst the boys of the Senior Class. It was the last day of the school year and for Patsy's class, the last day of compulsory education. Reddy Costello and Gurky Ryan could hardly contain the onslaught of joy they had felt from the moment they had got out of bed that morning. Last day or not, the boys queued in the school corridor at morning break, as they had done for the last seven years, to have their small bottle of fresh milk and the sliced bread corn beef sandwich.

If they were lucky, a number of boys would not want their sandwiches, which could mean a second sandwich for a hungry but astute pupil. Gurky Ryan was usually alert to such possibilities and took the opportunity to position himself in the corridor, while drinking his milk and eating his sandwich, so that he might observe simultaneously the declining stack of sandwiches and the shortening queue of pupils. The teacher on supervision duty would raise his cane above his head when he was certain all the pupils wishing to take food and drink had been served.

The raised cane signalled that boys could come and help themselves to "seconds", but woe betide the overeager, or the bargers and pushers, for then the cane was used across legs and backsides, and a painful stroke or two was all the extra nourishment the unfortunate boy would receive for his troubles. Gurky Ryan had long since mastered the art of perfect timing and invariably conveyed the strong impression to the supervising teacher that he was offering a service that prevented unnecessary wastefulness.

'Hoovering the place up again, are we, Master Ryan?' was the way Mr Bambrick put it.

Since his return to school after his release from hospital, Gurky had organised an assistant in the person of Dinny Fagan to help him in his daily feeding and drinking. His mutilated hand was still bandaged and confined to a sling and he realised he could not manage to eat the sandwich and drink the milk in the synchronised manner he preferred, without the use of two hands. Nor could he capture a second sandwich and hold on to what was already his, handicapped as he was.

For a very small fee, combined with vague but solemn promises of future rewards, never to be fulfilled, he persuaded Dinny to wolf down his own sandwich and drink and then to act as personal butler to Master Gurky Ryan Esq. This was no great hardship to Dinny as the younger pupils were served first thus making him available to minister to Gurky's needs. After a few days of trial and error and much moaning on Dinny's part, and one belt of the cane from an irate teacher, Dinny had the knack of securing a second sandwich for Gurky.

Working together under Gurky's tutelage both boys discovered a modus operandi that satisfied Gurky's needs.

'Stop moaning for Jaysus' sake,' pleaded Gurky. 'Just think about all the training I'm given you in looking after cripples. You'll be good for a job in a hospital when you leave school. You should be grateful to me, you should.'

They found the best way to achieve the results Gurky wanted when eating and drinking, was for Gurky to take the bottle of milk in his good left hand (Dinny having first removed the silver foil top) and take a mouthful from the bottle and swallow it, and while the taste of the milk and cream was still full in his throat, for Dinny to ram the sandwich between his teeth so he could take a "decent-sized-gobful", which was how Reddy Costello described it.

'Don't take the feckin thing away too fast,' Gurky complained to Dinny. 'You need to leave it in me mouth a bit longer so I'm not dropping bits all over the place and wasting it.'

'Stop complaining or you can shaggin do it yourself,' answered Dinny.

'There'll be no more after today, will there? Me last day in school, thank Jaysus in Heaven. Yis know what I mean, eh?'

'I wonder what old baldy ballocks Hayes wants to see us about?' Reddy Costello asked.

'Probably just wants to tell us he's glad to get rid of us and all, and we'll all end up in prison one day,' said Gurky. 'I don't give a shite so long as 3 o'clock comes and we're off.'

At 2.30, the leavers were assembled in their classroom with their teacher, Mr Bambrick. The headmaster, Mr Hayes, accompanied by the parish priest of St Anne's Church, Milltown, came into the classroom.

'Stand please, boys,' Mr Bambrick called.

'You may sit now, thank you,' said Mr Hayes. 'Father Fitzpatrick and I have come along to bid you all farewell and to wish you all every success in your future careers. I know some of you are continuing your education in colleges and high schools and others are starting to earn a living straight away. I hope your time in Milltown has been profitable, and for the most part, at least, enjoyable. If any boy has been unhappy, I am sorry, but I think such a boy must have been miserable to begin with. Father Fitzpatrick would like to say a few words to you, so I shall hand over to him now.'

'Well, boys,' the priest began, 'some of you no doubt have received the stick a good many times while you've been scholars here and I have no hesitation in saying you must have deserved it. I want you to remember that although, Mr Bambrick or Mr Hayes may have been actually holding the stick, it was Our Lord, Jesus Himself, who was wielding it. For your own sakes, boys, He wielded it with love, knocking the bad out of you, and making sure you stayed on the straight and narrow.'

'I want you all to remember that. Now bow your heads and I'll give you Our Lord's special blessing, and each of you make the sign of the cross and ask His forgiveness for all your sins.'

'I bet aul Bambo feels better that he didn't beat the shite out of us but *Jesus* did, and He did it because He loves you,' Reddy whispered to Patsy. 'Did you ever hear such a load of aul ballocks?'

When the headmaster and the parish priest left, Mr Bambrick had his class on his own for the last ten minutes of their last day.

'Well, you all heard the headmaster and Father Fitzpatrick. I hope when I caned you, it was because you deserved it, and I hope you're not going to hold a grudge against Our Lord. I want to wish you all well and I hope that whatever you're looking for when you leave here, you'll find it. I've enjoyed teaching you over the years, all of yous, even Reddy Costello and Master Gurky Ryan. You can stop sniggering.'

'They weren't the biggest pains in this class, were they, Master Browne? What words have I got for you? I suppose I could do a Mr Welsh and quote some Shakespeare. *Hamlet* would do nicely I suppose, where Polonius—he's the father of Laertes, one of Hamlet's pals—what's Polonius famous for, Master Fagan?'

'When Laertes is going away for a couple of years to live in Paris, Polonius—that's his da—gives him an awful load of advice about borrowing cash and lending things and all.'

'That's what me own Da says to me all the time,' chimed in Gurky Ryan.

'Very good, Master Fagan,' continued Mr Bambrick. 'There's real hope for you. Well, I'm not Polonius and you are not characters from *Hamlet*, though I can imagine one or two of you becoming clowns and fools; no need to take offence, Reddy Costello; by "fools" I mean court jesters. There may even be a gravedigger amongst you, what do you think, Master Browne? Don't bother to answer. That's called a rhetorical question.'

'Oh that's very good, Sir,' said Gurky Ryan, without any clue of what his schoolmaster was talking about but having some notion that Noel Browne was on the receiving end of a telling off.

'Shut up, Ryan, it's not yet too late to say goodbye to the stick. Now what I do want to say is this: I think it's very important that you discover heroes. By heroes, I mean people you can admire, people who inspire you and that you would like to be like. It doesn't matter whether your heroes are men or women or whether they're alive or dead.'

'What matters is they've done some real good for the world, for humanity, and you recognise the good and great things they've done, and they make you feel that you'd like to be like them and want to try to do similar great things, even if only in a small way. I hope I'm making sense to you because all of us, especially you leaving school today, need a guiding light, like they say, "a star to sail your ship by". Do you understand? Yes, Fagan, what is it?'

'Who is your hero, Sir?'

'We're talking about your heroes not mine, but it's a fair question. I've always admired Jim Larkin who was a trade union leader during the great Dublin lockout in 1912. Also, Florence Nightingale, the famous nurse with the lamp. When you read what she did in the hospital at Scutari during the Crimean War, you can't help but admire her and feel her greatness. Our own Michael Collins was a brave man and a strong leader. Strangely enough, the British wartime Prime Minister, Winston Churchill, was an enthusiastic admirer of Collins.'

'Go on, Sir! Who else?' Reddy Costello shouted.

'My own father,' said Mr Bambrick. 'A man who worked hard all his life to bring up a large family. Always wheeling and dealing, never really knowing what the next day would bring, but he always had a smile for you. Enough of that now. But don't forget heroes come in many shapes and sizes, and they can come just as easily from books or films or legends; think of Robin Hood or Cuchulain, they don't have to be real people; or even… are you listening, young Gurky? The fastest gun in the Wild West.'

'Over the coming years, boys, I'll meet you time and again, and the first question I'll ask each of you is: who are your heroes? I do hope you'll have some.'

Chapter 20

Geraldine Quinn was at last persuaded to "walk out" with Reddy Costello but the conditions were stringent. They were to be together during the daylight hours so there would be no "hanky panky after dark", as her father put it. They had to be "in company" and "not just the two of them getting up to God knows what", was how her mother put it.

Poor Reddy, poor Geraldine; they stood side by side in the front room of the Quinn household, what the Quinn parents called "The Parlour", to listen to and nod assent to the litany of allowables and forbiddens, recited by Geraldine's parents in the manner of Greek Tragedy declamation.

Reddy was reflecting how much better it might have been had he fallen for Angela Barry, the newsagent's daughter. She was free to go out with whomever she liked and her parents seemed to be quite content to leave the tricky world of young romance entirely with the young themselves.

With some effort and pain, Reddy organised an outing for his two closest pals, Patsy and Gurky, who asked Catherine and Eileen to join them on an excursion to Dublin city centre where they would picnic in St Stephen's Green. They could be away all day and would not have to return home until, 'At least 10 o'clock cause it'll still be daylight,' Reddy stated with some certainty.

Alas, Reddy had not counted on codicils being added to the established proscription.

'You'll have her back here at 8 o'clock at the latest so she can have her cocoa and brush her teeth before she sits down to her reading. What would she be doing out until 10 o'clock, for goodness sake?'

Patsy insisted they walked from Landscape to St Stephen's Green rather than take the bus.

'You always want to shaggin walk,' said Gurky. 'I don't understand you half the time.'

'What do you want to understand? The weather is gorgeous and we can go down through Orwell, Rathgar, Rathmines and over the canal. We can look in the shops and see all the buildings and smell the different bits of the city. And when we get there we'll have great appetites.'

'I don't need to do anything to make me appetite great. Do you not see enough of Dublin? I think you need your feckin head testing.'

In the end, all five were happy to indulge Patsy and walk the three and a half miles into Dublin centre, and at least four of them knew they would have a running commentary on streets, buildings, army barracks, parks, cinemas and any spot at all that had significance for any member of the Fagan family. They insisted, however, that they would catch the number 14 bus from Dolier St to Churchtown when they were ready to come home.

Patsy was reluctant to agree at first, but with Reddy holding him in a headlock, Gurky pulling with all his might on one ear lobe and Catherine tickling him mercilessly, the promise was extracted, repeated and finally repeated again, preambled with the words, "I swear on the memory of Robert Emmet that I, Patsy Fagan…"

'And when we go past the Stella picture house,' said Reddy, 'if you tell us again that's where your Da met your Ma for their first date back in 1941 and they were married two months later, I'll strangle you. Do you hear?'

Patsy managed to restrain himself sufficiently so as not to invoke the wrath of Reddy or Gurky, but yet he was as ever enthusiastic when he could show his friends something about Dublin, a building or place where some noteworthy event had happened. They had reached the Grand Canal and the old Portobello Harbour on the Rathmines Rd.

'Come over here onto Portobello Bridge,' cried Patsy, 'there's something I want to show yous.'

'Oh my Jaysus, I thought it was too shaggin good to last,' said Gurky.

'Is this the place he nearly drowned?' Geraldine Quinn asked.

'Sometimes I wish he had feckin drowned,' answered Reddy. 'But no, it wasn't here.'

'Reddy Costello! What a shocking thing to say and you'd better not use language like that in front of my father or he'll skin you alive. I'm interested, Patsy, even if certain people are not.'

'That's telling you now good and proper, you Smart-Alec,' jeered Gurky. 'Jaysus, that Geraldine sort of grows on you, doesn't she? I'm dead interested as well, Patsy Fagan. Won't you please tell me all about it so long as it hasn't got anything to do with churches or Protestants or bishops and all that. I'm not like that bold Reddy who's just a gobshite. I'm a nice fella wanting to learn about every class of thing under the sun.'

'I hope you're not making fun of me, Gurky Ryan,' said Geraldine Quinn, the colour of her face almost matching her flaming red hair. 'Because if you are, I'll give your ears a good boxing.'

'Not me, Geraldine, not me. I'd never do that. Do yis know what I mean?'

'Come on over here,' called Patsy laughing. 'I shouldn't really be laughing at all cause what I want to show yous is very sad. Look down into the canal lock there. You see, it's very deep and dark. Well, about a hundred years ago, a horse-drawn tram was travelling along here full of people. For some reason, nobody was able to say why, the horses reared up and bolted and the tram with all the people on it toppled over into the lock.'

'Oh my God,' said Catherine. 'Were any people killed?'

'Yes,' answered Patsy. 'Four people and a baby drowned. The rest managed to get out or were saved by people who were standing around the bridge at the time.'

'Well, that's a nice cheerful little tale,' said Eileen. 'Can we go on down to Stephen's Green and get something to eat before we all get sick?'

'I think we should say a prayer for their poor souls first,' said Geraldine.

'Oh me sweet Jaysus's Mother, pray for me,' groaned Reddy.

They bought fresh milk, bread, and sliced ham in a shop at Kelly's Corner. Gurky and Reddy went to one of the street dealers in Camden St and bought some apples and oranges. With their brown bags of provisions, they made their way along Harcourt St and entered Stephen's Green through the main gates on its northwest corner.

Catherine and Eileen between them had brought butter, knives, and some enamel plates, and soon the party of six were relaxed on the grass enjoying ham sandwiches and fresh fruit washed back with fresh milk straight from the cold bottles passed from hand to hand and mouth to mouth.

'Just imagine,' said Reddy, wiping the milk off his mouth with the back of his hand, 'we never have to go to school again…that is unless you want to.'

'When are you going to start work, Reddy?' Eileen asked him.

'Me Da says I can take me time for two or three weeks just having finished school. Have a sort of holiday he said so I can get meself ready for big changes in me life. It's either going to be a milkman or working with your cousin, Billy O'Hara.'

'And what about you, Gurky? Now you've lost a finger and a bit of your thumb, what are you planning to do?'

'I don't know yet, Eileen. Just go in somewhere and ask the man for a job.'

'What do you mean, Gurky?' Geraldine asked. 'Have you no plans about what you want to do, what sort of work you'd like?'

'Nope. Just go up to the man and say you want a job. Doesn't matter what job so long as you get the money at the end of the week. Just ask the man and say please and thank you. That's what me Da says.'

'Are you leaving school, Geraldine, or carrying on?' Patsy asked.

'Oh, I'm continuing with the Sacred Heart Nuns in Mount Anville Rd.'

'And what do you want to do when you eventually leave for good?'

'Don't know for definite yet. I've thought about nursing or even becoming a nun and going to the missions as a nurse.'

'Oh sweet loving Mother of God,' whimpered Reddy.

'That's what I'd like to do, said Eileen, 'become a nurse. But I've still got a year left in St Anne's in Milltown. And after that, I don't know where I'll go to school. Maybe join Catherine and Patsy in Sandymount.'

'I did think about something that I'd like to be,' Gurky called, sounding excited. 'If I had me choice that is.'

'What?' They asked.

'Like aul Bambo said, everybody needs heroes, so there must be a shortage of heroes, so that's what I'd like to be, a hero.'

'And a damned fine hero you'd make, Gurky Ryan,' said Catherine. 'What's this your famous Mr Bambrick has been saying to yous?'

'He wants us to have heroes and all,' said Reddy. 'Makes you feckin sick.'

'Who's your hero, Reddy?' Geraldine asked.

'The one and only. The King…have you guessed? Yeah, it's got to be Elvis!'

'But he's not really a hero, is he?' Geraldine said.

'What do you mean, not a hero? There's millions of people queue up to see him at the pictures. Not like that aul fella Robert what's his name Emmet. You don't see anybody lining up to see him, do you?'

'Could it be because we don't know where he's buried, you amadan?' Patsy answered, determined not to rise to Reddy's bait.

'Do girls have heroes?' Gurky asked.

'Of course they do, you eegit,' Eileen answered.

'Yeah, but I bet they're all men, film stars and singers and all,' stated a cocky Reddy.

'No they're not, Smarty-Pants,' said Geraldine angrily.

'Who are yours then? Quick, answer now and don't try and think about loads of women and all,' insisted Reddy.

'I don't have to think about it at all,' said Geraldine in her most haughty manner. 'I have always—and certainly before I knew you, Reddy Costello—admired the nun in the film *The Bells of St Mary's*, so there.'

'I'm sorry I asked. Can you not think about anything except shaggin nuns?'

'If you use dirty language one more time, I won't talk to you again. And for your information, there's lots of women heroes, like St Bernadette of Lourdes and St Therese of Lisieux, and St Veronica who wiped the face of Jesus.'

'But they're all nuns,' cried an increasingly despairing Reddy, painfully aware that any chance of a bit of kissing with Geraldine before the day was out was fast disappearing down the drain.

'Ah, you got that wrong about St Veronica,' shouted Gurky joyously.

'What?' Reddy asked.

'She wasn't a nun. Nuns wasn't invented then when Our Lord was on the planet. Anyway, how could she be a nun when she was a woman baking in sin?'

'Taken in sin, Gurky, not "baking",' whispered Catherine helpfully.

'Well, I don't see anything wrong with having men heroes,' declared Eileen, 'even if you're a girl. I have men heroes if you want to know.'

'Good girl, Eileen,' said Reddy. 'I always knew you had a soft spot for Elvis.'

'You know where you can stick Elvis, Reddy Costello. But I don't mind telling you that that Pat Boone is fine, especially when he sings "Love letters in the Sand". So is Audie Murphy who was a real hero during the war. He was the most decorated American soldier for the whole of the Second World War. Now I think he's my favourite hero.'

'We haven't heard who Catherine's heroes are,' said Patsy.

'I love lots of the ones you've already mentioned.'

'But who are your own special ones?' Patsy asked.

'You know at least one, Patsy Fagan, but you just want me to say it. All right then, ever since you lent me the book, one of my favourite people in history is Anne Frank. Will that do you now?'

'You haven't said a man hero, Catherine,' said Gurky blushing slightly.

'I must admit, Gurky, that I do like Shane,' smiled Catherine. 'I also admire Patrick Pearse for his courage and willingness to die for Ireland's independence, though I would've preferred he'd lived. And my great women heroes or heroines, if you prefer, are Countess Markievicz and Emily Pankhurst.'

'I don't know them,' said Gurky. 'Do the rest of yis know them?'

'The first one, the Countess, fought for Ireland,' answered Catherine, 'and the second one, Emily, fought for women.'

'There's always someone fighting for shaggin Ireland,' yawned Reddy.

'What did you say, Reddy Costello?' Geraldine demanded.

'Eh, nothing, Geraldine, nothing at all.'

'Well, I know who me best heroes are now,' said Gurky. 'I was thinkin' about it after Bambo's last class with us. Do yis want to know?'

'Yes,' answered the three girls.

'Yis promise not to laugh?'

'Of course we won't laugh,' said Eileen. 'Come on, tell us!'

'Well, I went through all me comics and I put them into three piles. One pile was good heroes, the second pile was gooder heroes and the third pile was best heroes.'

'Who was in the best pile?' Patsy asked.

'I had Kit Carson and Buck Jones and the Lone Ranger and Tonto, and Lash Larue, I think he's great. And I had Dan Dare from The Eagle, you know, and Desperate Dan from The Dandy. But me favourite of the lot is not in any comic and Catherine's already said him, it's Shane.'

'But how are you going to be a hero, Gurky?' Catherine asked him gently.

'Well, you see I couldn't think of a single hero that has a finger and a bit of his thumb missing, so I'm going to write. I've been practising with the three fingers I've got left on me hand and it's OK, not perfect by any means but it'll be game ball one day—what was I telling yis, oh yeah, so I'm going to write a new comic about a cowboy who goes around all the towns in the Wild West doing good, like aul Bambo said.

'The thing is he's got to be different from the other cowboy heroes, like Shane was. He's not going to be just after bank robbers and murderers and all that class of thing.'

'What's he going to be like?' an excited Catherine asked.

'He's going to go around helping the down-and-outs, like the ones that had to go to the Standing Up Doss House that Patsy told us about. And he'll protect cripples and anyone who comes into town in a wheelchair. He's not a sissy or anything. He'll be a very fast draw and any aul slags who think he's a sissy will soon find out their mistake.'

'I think that's wonderful, Gurky,' said Catherine.

'And I'm going to call him Billy Three Fingers. That's how I'll be a hero. In the comics.'

Chapter 21

On a very hot and sunny afternoon a week after the excursion to St Stephen's Green, Patsy and his brother, Dinny, were sitting on the bank of the River Dodder, just below the weir on the Rathfarnham Rd. They were fishing for trout, or as Dinny put it "for anything at all that bites me bait". Dinny was using earthworms on a size 4 hook. His rod was a six-foot bamboo cane of the type used for propping up runner beans in a garden.

He had no reel and most of his line was butcher's string with the last four or five feet of nylon fishing line onto which he had tied his hook. He had used a one-inch diameter copper washer as a weight tied and knotted just above the nylon. He was concentrating intently as he was convinced he had a number of bites, and that at any moment a wild brown trout would make his bamboo rod jump off its rest, such would be the force of the fish's take.

Patsy was better equipped. He had a split cane nine-foot two-piece rod with a second-hand Mitchell 300 reel that his uncle Jack had given him as a birthday present. His line was made of the most modern nylon of 2lb weight. He had fixed a quarter ounce lead leger on a free running swivel and had tightened his line until the tip of his rod just began to bend to the weight. Unlike Dinny, he had no expectation of a sudden jerking on the line and further bending of his rod.

He had changed his worm three times already and had also reduced his hook from a size 6 to 10 but without attracting a single bite so far. He knew it was folly to fish in such bright sunlight.

'I think the fish are on holidays, just like us,' he said to Dinny.

'Shush,' said Dinny. 'I've just had another bite. Just be quiet, I'm trying to concentrate.'

'It's too hot and sunny. We should've waited till tonight.'

'Shut up will you! I've got something interested in me worm.'

Patsy was feeling a little guilty about going fishing when he believed he could have been useful in his father's garage, but Tom Fagan had told him to have "one or two weeks holidays and not to worry too much about the garage". He encouraged his son to play football or go fishing or visit "your mad cousin, Billy O'Hara".

He was enjoying the long summer days and the hours of freedom that had no timetable. His books were all ready for September and Sandymount, and he had already started to scratch the surface of new school subjects but felt frustrated that while he could look at French words, he had no clue how to say them. A harsh voice broke into his daydreams.

'Ah, there y'are, Patsy Fagan. What are you up to? How's your brother, Dinny? No more shite in the trousers I pray?'

It was Mr Brophy out for his "constitutional". "Good for you after eating, you know".

'I'm here fishing and minding me own business as even a blind man could see, Mr Brophy,' Patsy answered, blushing at the embarrassing memories.

'Ah, sure you are. I hope your mammy and dad are fine. Give them my best regards now.'

Miserable ballocks. Always wanting to jeer at something. How many times did he always manage to be passing here when poor Dinny just couldn't hold it in. Anyway, that's when he was just a kid, don't know when the last time even was; think he was about ten. Always somebody wants to remind you. Glad Catherine wasn't here with us. I'd have died cause that aul ballocks would've said it just the same even if she was here sat beside me.

'Patsy! I've got something to tell you.'

It was Reddy Costello running along the Dodder bank shouting and waving.

'This is feckin useless,' said Dinny. 'First aul dry shite Brophy and now that gormless eegit, Reddy Costello. There's no peace around here. How can you be expected to catch fish with all this racket going on? I'm moving about a hundred miles up the river. Give us a call when you're going home, will you?'

'What's all the commotion?' Patsy asked as Reddy sat down beside him.

He could see Reddy's face was blotchy and his eyes red as though he had been crying.

'What's the matter?'

'Me Da told us this morning that we have to move to England. We're going in about two weeks.'

'You never said anything about going to England before,' answered Patsy.

'I didn't know. Da says that's what he meant when he told me to have a holiday and get ready for big changes in me life.'

'But why are yous going?'

'Me da's found a job as a long-distance lorry driver that pays good money. He says we can't afford to live in Dublin any more cause he can't make enough money to pay for everything.'

'But with you starting work and all, wouldn't that make a difference?'

'I'm starting work OK, building feckin ships in Newcastle or Sunderland or some shaggin place. But the worst is I can't even start working yet.'

'What do you mean?'

'I have to go to fuckin school for another year. They go on a year longer in England. You have to be feckin fifteen. Did you ever hear anything like it. Jaysus Christ, I'm right ballocksed!'

Reddy was crying and leant against his friend who was also crying. Patsy was not sure whether he was crying because Reddy Costello was so upset or because he was losing a friend, or because his own fears for his father's position were never far away.

'But it's not all bad,' Patsy said trying to cheer up his friend. 'You need another year at school,' he joked, 'to make up for all the things you didn't learn.'

'Fuck off'

'And if you're going to work in a shipyard, you'll learn a trade, won't you?'

'Just sat here looking at this river makes me feel fuckin seasick. What do I want to be building ships for?'

'You'll also be able to see all those football teams you're always going on about: Arsenal, Manchester United, Everton. They all play at Newcastle, don't they?'

'Yeah, that's right. Maybe I'll be able to see Jackie Milburn, Stanley Matthews and Tom Finney, you never know, do you?'

'And you'll be able to go and see Marty Wilde and Tommy Steel and maybe even Elvis will come to England. You could be lucky.'

'Yeah,' said Reddy, becoming excited. 'Maybe it won't be too bad at that.'

They walked home, each with an arm around the other's shoulder, Patsy carrying his rod neatly in one hand, and Dinny following behind, not a fish to be seen.

'Just the same,' said Reddy when they arrived home, 'I wish we didn't have to go.'

I went down to the docks on the North Wall of the Liffey to say goodbye to Reddy and all the family. They were sailing to Liverpool on a car ferry at 8 o'clock in the morning. Everybody up in Landscape had been going around to their house all week saying goodbye and wishing them well and all. Ma and Da went to see Mr and Mrs Costello and took their address in Newcastle and promised to write and keep in touch and everything.

Da got me up at 6 o'clock and you could feel the heat in the air even that early. I asked Reddy if we could go down together but he said he had to stay with his Ma and Da to help with the younger kids. I left the house at 6:30 and rode down on my bike so I could get there in plenty of time before the boat sailed. The roads were empty, not a car or bike in sight. Tony wrote in a letter home that it was a big difference between England and Ireland.

"People get up really early in Coventry and all over England, and you have to be in work at 7:30. If you're more than three minutes late, you lose quarter of an hour's pay. The roads are full of cars, bikes and motorbikes. You've never seen so many motorbikes and everybody rushing off to work."

It's gas really because in Dublin, the roads don't get really busy until about 8 o'clock in the morning. Tony said we're a "later country" than England: "Our pictures start later in the evening and our pubs close later, and Irish people go to bed later and get out of bed later." He seems to have really settled in Coventry. Ma and Da miss him a lot—we all do really—but I can't see him coming back, unless it was for a girl.

Terrible to see Reddy's ma, Mrs Costello, looking very upset, holding two babies in her arms and Reddy's sister, Teresa, pushing the pram up the gangplank onto the boat. The men loading the cars and vans wouldn't let them put the pram on the roof of the car, saying it was too big and all, and they'd just have to take the pram on board with them and one of them would have to wheel it off when they got to Liverpool, and then they could put it back on the roof of the car for the rest of the journey.

They had an old 1938 Vauxhall 14 and you could see it was packed with stuff.
All the clothes were bundled up in bed sheets and tied with a big knot. The
bundles were spread on the back seat of the car and the older kids, including
Reddy, had to get in there on top of the bundles and flatten them down, and then
their Da passed the smaller children in to sit on their laps. Every inch of the car
was full. There were pots and pans and delft jammed into every corner and on
the floor and under the front seats.

They'd put the suitcase and every class of other bag they could find in the
boot and on the roof rack. By the time they put the pram on, the whole lot was
about ten foot high. No wonder they took the pram off, and there was no room in
it for the baby anyway because it was packed with shoes and knives, forks, spoons
and cups, and some bottles of milk and loaves of bread.

The ticket man let me go on to help carry some bits and pieces that fell off
the pram and to say goodbye to them all. Reddy came back to the gangplank with
me but we didn't say much. I told him I'd write and I joked about him learning
something in his posh English school. He laughed when I told him that Tony had
written to me ("don't show Ma and Da what I've written!") saying that English
girls were mad for Irish fellas.

"Jaysus, maybe I'll be busy then getting in a bit of kissing practice, eh?" He
told me Geraldine Quinn had come around to see him to say goodbye and she'd
given him a big kiss.

"You're joking," I said.

"No, she was all tears and saying she was sorry for scolding me every minute
of the day and she wished we could go out again."

He was stood on the deck waving to me as the ship set sail. I watched the
water churning up as the propeller turned, brown and muddy and rusty. I
couldn't see him anymore because the sun was shining in my eyes and there were
seagulls flying everywhere and screaming and diving and looking for food. I
turned around to go out and find my bike and I saw Geraldine Quinn standing
in a corner, wearing a blue frock and open sandals. She had a blue and white
striped ribbon holding her long red hair in a ponytail.

"Hello, Geraldine."

"Hello, Patsy. I came to say goodbye but I got here too late and the boat was
in the middle of the river. I waved like mad but I don't know if he saw me. The
sun was blinding me and I couldn't see."

"I'm sure he knew you were here, Geraldine," I told her. She looked at me and I could see was crying a little.

"I wonder if we'll ever see him again," she said.

The great day had arrived: Monday 8 September 1958. Here I am at last in Sandymount. The bike ride in was fine with the sun shining and everything but it'll be different in the rain. Still, it won't be too bad, I hope. Easy to see who the new ones are, like me. New blazer with the school badge standing out like clean headlamps on a motor car. The older fellas and girls look very cosy with each other.

They're not looking round at everything the way we are, like we've been just born; they're just strolling in, books under their arms, no bags or cases. We must stand out like sore thumbs. Like me, stupid enough to have a school satchel for Christ's sake, on my back with the straps clipped together across my chest, like a kid going to baby school. Thanks be to Jesus, there's lots of other eegits like me.

I spotted Catherine when I came in the gates carrying a briefcase sort of bag. I can't let her see my satchel and I'll have to find something different for tomorrow. I'm not sure about wearing this feckin cap either. I'm like one of the kids in Goodbye Mr Chips. Never thought when I was watching the film that I'd be wearing one of the caps one day. Funny what you never think about. You'd think looking around at all these students (that's what they call us) that you were in another country. They all **look** so different from the kids in Milltown.

Their haircuts are not the same, posher Tony would say, and not just because there are girls here, but the boys as well are different. They're cleaner and look healthy, and they sort of have a shine about them, on their skin and in their hair and all. You can **smell** the soap off them when you're standing up close. Do I smell of soap? Do I look like them? I do and me arse! Just look at that little group over there, Catherine with them.

All of them new like me. Catherine looks like them; I don't mean all pretty with lovely long hair and all, but they've got the same kind of shine about them. I hope I'm like them.

Classes of boys and girls together, I can't believe my luck. The first teacher we had, he's our "Tutor", told us where to sit and gave us our timetables. I'm sat next to a boy called Finbar. He wears big glasses and looks very clever but

174

he's got a nice smile and he's already given me a mint. "Keeps your breath fresh," he said.

Good idea that, keep your breath fresh, in case you get a chance to give one or two of these girls a kiss. I'm only joking for crying out loud. I'd rather kiss Catherine than anybody else. Pity she's sat right at the back where I can't see her easily.

We have all these different teachers for different lessons. Mr Gallagher, our Tutor, teaches us geography. Then we had Miss Naughton—she's gorgeous—for French. She smiled at me and I nearly dropped dead when she asked if I could make sure to collect in the homework books next lesson. Homework! Would you believe it? Reddy and Gurky would have a fit. I've never had homework in my life before but I know Catherine got it every night in the Loretto Convent.

After the French, there was geometry and algebra. The only disappointment so far was the dozy ballocks we had for Roman History. He's an ex-monk or something but as soon as he started talking, you began to fall asleep. I'd change him any day for Mr Bambrick. We had a visit from the headmaster's missis and the bell for The Angelus rang when she was talking to us. "I'll say The Angelus with you, boys and girls, if you would all like to stand up."

She was just like Sister Carmel used to be, a sort of smile on her face as if saying The Angelus was like eating a nice bit of chocolate and you were really going to enjoy it.

"The angel of the Lord declared unto Mary, and she conceived by the Holy Ghost."

Finbar next to me nearly choked when he heard me say, "And she can sleep with the Holy Ghost." Course, I wasn't thinking about it. It just came out, even though I've been saying it right for years. The very best thing of the whole of that first day was when we had our first English lesson in the afternoon. I knew when I saw Mr O'Connor I was going to like him. He was tall and handsome with very dark hair and blue eyes—what my Ma would call "striking".

He was wearing a charcoal-grey suit with a very dark red tie and blue shirt and he walked with a slight spring in his step as if his dark brown suede shoes made him bounce a little as he went along. Anyway, in that first lesson, he told us what we would be studying in English, and I nearly had a stroke when he was telling us what Shakespeare we'd be reading during the term.

"I wonder," he said, "if any of you have come across Romeo and Juliet. *We'll be reading it in class but I am hoping we will be able to produce the play early in the spring term for the rest of the school and parents. I shall be auditioning in the next month for a cast and I hope we have lots of boys and girls coming forward to read. Do you think we might have in this class a boy and a girl who could play the parts of Romeo and Juliet?" I turned around and smiled at Catherine.*

The End